THE MODERN FORAGER'S COOKBOOK

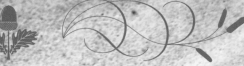

Rob Connoley

PHOTOGRAPHS BY JAY HEMPHILL

CONTRIBUTIONS BY ANDREA FEUCHT

THE MODERN FORAGER'S COOKBOOK

Recipes from the Farm, Forest, Field, and Stream

SKYHORSE PUBLISHING

Skyhorse Publishing books may be purchased in bulk at special discounts for sales promotion, corporate gifts, fund-raising, or educational purposes. Special editions can also be created to specifications. For details, contact the Special Sales Department, Skyhorse Publishing, 307 West 36th Street, 11th Floor, New York, NY 10018 or info@skyhorsepublishing.com.

Skyhorse® and Skyhorse Publishing® are registered trademarks of Skyhorse Publishing, Inc.®, a Delaware corporation.

Visit our website at www.skyhorsepublishing.com.

10 9 8 7 6 5 4 3 2 1

Library of Congress Cataloging-in-Publication Data is available on file.

Cover design by Kai Texel
Interior design by Laura Klynstra
Cover photo by Jay Hemphill
Edited by Nicole Frail

Print ISBN: 978-1-5107-7647-0
Ebook ISBN: 978-1-5107-7917-4

Printed in China

IN MEMORIAM

Mina Yamashita
The champion of all champions

Steven Shaw
Without whom this book would not exist

CONTENTS

Section 1:
FORAGING, ETHICS & THE BUILDING OF A RESTAURANT: RE-VISIONING THE FOOD WE EAT

Section 2:
FROM THE FOREST (ANIMALS)

Section 3:
FROM THE FARM (DOMESTIC PLANTS)

Section 4:

FROM THE FIELD (WILD PLANTS)

Section 5:

GARNISH AND FLAIR RECIPES

FOREWORD

by Andrea Feucht

"I could be wrong. But I'm not." —CHEF ROB CONNOLEY, early 2014

It's a recent evening in late spring, in a modest home in Silver City, New Mexico. The dining room table is flanked with papers (mostly bills) and a laptop, but each place setting holds a plate of Salad Niçoise, garnished with pickled onions, freshly steamed asparagus, and tender Italian tuna. The chef serving this meal is not Rob Connoley of the Curious Kumquat, but rather his partner in life and cooking adventures, Tyler Connoley. Both of them are critiquing the tinned tuna and the doneness of the asparagus, as they are wont to do, with the caring that comes out of passion. Just as many happy friendships involve a little bickering, so goes the relationship with a chef and his dishes.

When they met, Tyler was a capable gourmet home cook and Rob, a curious international dabbler; the desire and ability to cook from scratch was mutual. After they moved to Silver City, both worked full time, but Rob's kitchen tinkering grew into a life of its own at the inspiration of a "little" online community called eGullet. He participated in pastry challenges and discussed his life in a small town as a self-taught cook. All the while the makings of the Curious Kumquat were taking root.

Like countless businesses before it, the Curious Kumquat came from real problems begging for solutions. First, Rob's lament was, "I can't buy good cheese in Silver City." The Cut the Cheese Club began in 1999, giving Rob a means to gather enough folks together to buy fancy cheeses so he'd be able to justify buying some himself. Other gourmet ingredients followed, and Rob had himself a little store in 2002. In 2006, the Curious Kumquat became a full-blown gourmet grocery in its own renovated building, supplying hot giardiniera and chestnuts in syrup to customers all over the region. Before long, Rob added prepared foods and cooking classes to the offerings.

Around this time, I "met" Rob via eGullet—enjoying both his well-documented experiments, like meat-based desserts, and his writing in general. One day, I finally noticed he was *in New Mexico*—just like me. Despite being four hours away, I was suddenly excited and wanted to meet this dude. He was just beginning to serve café food at the store; I made the trip down to meet him and take cooking classes. I wondered how to write his story to really show him off to the culinary world.

While enjoying the local community and surrounding wild lands (which included the Gila Wilderness) and brainstorming ingredients, something clicked in Rob's head. He says, "I recognized that the Apaches were here for a long, long time and didn't head south for the winter. That's when I realized there must be plenty of food year-round in the Gila." Once Rob learned from local mentors (see Building a Foraging Team, p. 26), he began to transform his menu, beginning with experimental dinners several times per year. These events were a win-win for everyone involved. Fans were happy to fork over a lump of cash for anything Rob had up his sleeve, no questions asked. Rob took that confidence (and money) and blew his creative wad on crazy experiments like beet caviar or clay-packed bison sweetbreads with pickled juniper berries. We all loved it.

Except for the headcheese. Don't ask about that.

Back in the café, regular three-course tasting dinners were added in 2010, using techniques and inspiration gathered from the experimental dinners.

Rob's goal of becoming a one-man revolution in modernist cuisine was always on his mind. A tiny town like Silver City had just as much reason to have a nationally recognized restaurant as any other place. Period.

Even in those rarest of recipes that don't turn out how Rob wants, you'll find excitement. There are things to learn, flavor components to rejigger and tweak, and all of us are along for the delicious ride. Declare your belief in Rob's cookery on the edge by fastening your safety belt and stepping toward the ledge . . .

INTRODUCTION

The phone rings in my restaurant kitchen. I answer in a loud voice to overpower the racket of compressors and fans: "I'm busy, what's up?"

The voice on the other end says, "I've caught a raccoon." Awkward pause. "Interested?"

How the hell did I become the collector for every piece of crap, living or dead, that gets pulled out of the forest? I didn't sign on to be the clean-up team at wildlife murder scenes, and I certainly don't want to be your dirt-shoveling gardener. But I grit my teeth and say, "Sure. I'll take it."

And such is the life of a modern foraged food chef. In a country that thinks foraging means dumpster diving, and most guests are sure you're doing it to save a few pennies on ingredients, I've been correcting the misguided notions of both customers and fellow chefs for years.

Foraging is in fashion right now, and as with many past culinary fads and movements, exciting dishes and techniques are flooding into the mainstream faster than can be consumed. Moments after a guest eats a plate of lichen and urchin at Copenhagen's NOMA, photos pour through Instagram and Facebook. Within days, chefs and home cooks across the globe are rushing to copy the latest and greatest dish. Even stolid, tradition-bound chefs are at least finding wild herbs or flowers to adorn their plates. As a chef who has created modernist foraged cuisine for a number of years, I've chosen to dig deep into this genre—and illogically in the middle of the high desert of New Mexico.

The odd feature about the foraging fad is that it's millennia old. Europeans have been traipsing through the woods, raking through rotting leaves for morels and porcini, from the time of epicurean Romans. The Apaches, whose ancestral lands also provide my bounty, have been foraging as long as the Europeans . . . yet for them, it was survival, not flair. Foraging is neither a fad nor a movement; it is a refocusing on what humans have done from the start of time.

I believe it is important that we understand where modern chefs fit into the history of the foraging tradition, if for no other reason than to acknowledge our link to the foragers who preceded us. If we don't have that connection, our foraging can easily ramble into dangerous territories of environmental disrespect, theft, or even diner illness.

My own path to foraging began when I served a locally raised tomato in January a number of years ago. My restaurant was rooted in the locavore movement, serving all manner of foods found within an hour of my kitchen. And I had served hot-house tomatoes for quite some time, until the night when, on a whim, I ate a freshly cut wedge. The lack of flavor, the tough skin, the slightly mealy texture—a tomato surely shunned by every Italian grandmother. And that sent me down an existential rabbit hole.

Why local? Why organic? Why fair trade? Do we really know why we eat these foods? As my skepticism grew, as did my search for clarity, my thoughts moved to propriety. Yes, we can eat locally-grown tomatoes in January, but should we? Do I eat a tomato in January because it's good, or simply because I can? Why eat a substandard tomato when I can harvest fresh watercress from a mountain spring? What did our ancestors eat in January? (A hint: there's a reason our culture tosses up so many cured meats, canned vegetables, pickles, and such.)

So I dug deeper. My restaurant is in the historic land of the Apaches. Geronimo hunted on the very land where I gather. They did not pick hothouse tomatoes in January, yet they survived. And so I evolved my restaurant's menu to focus on historic Apache diets. No, not fry bread and mutton, but even more historic. Reading the research on items found in archaeological digs, I developed an Athabaskan shopping list that the Apaches might have followed. And while this research provided twenty or so ingredients, I suspected there were more.

I began watching what local fauna consumed . . . and what they did not. I reached out to a local "mountain man," Doug Simons, who had lived exclusively off the land for years and had been taught about the plants of our area and the benefits and risks of each. I became enamored of the abundant hackberry (dried on the tree, they taste like dates) and learned the folly of trying to gather wild strawberries before the bears got to them. I was continually testing my harvesting practices to ensure that the plants would produce

in the future, my customers would be nourished by the food, and I could use the ingredient to excite the modern palate.

Parallel to my explorations, I read about my peers: those who "forage" the edges of vineyards tainted with pesticides and who gather dandelion greens from abandoned lots dusted with chemicals from razed buildings. I've chatted with numerous chefs about where they gather their food, almost always hearing that their foraging areas are "secret." But if the area is safe enough to serve the food, and prolific enough to yield ingredients sustainably, shouldn't a chef be able to publish the location of his harvest on the menu? And, more importantly, shouldn't his guests have the right to know where their food is coming from?

These are big questions, ones that challenge the high-roller restaurants featuring foraged foods. Yet this book is not about challenging. Rather, it's about encouraging both the chef and the home cook to get outside, enjoy the bounty that is in all of our backyards, and prepare that bounty in ways that can intrigue the palate. I hope you'll enjoy this collection of my work. Every acorn I gather and every cattail I pluck is now presented for you to enjoy. Cheers!

HOW TO USE THIS BOOK

WEIGHTS & MEASURES

This book includes both weight (both US and UK) and volume measures. In our kitchen, we use weight primarily, opting for grams for ease and precision. In the writing of the recipes, modifications have often been made for ease of measure as long as it does not affect the outcome of the recipe. For example, a recipe may call for 2 tablespoons of butter, which is technically 28 grams, but we have rounded it to 30 grams for easier use. As with all recipes, minor adjustments such as these rarely have a noticeable impact.

OUR RECIPE DESIGNATIONS EXPLAINED

We designate each recipe by season, difficulty, and whether the primary ingredients are foraged, farmed plants, or animals.

Seasons are generally Spring, Summer, Fall, or Winter, but there are often ingredients that will cross over by season. If you are using online or purchased substitutions, you will be able to ignore seasonality.

Difficulty is shown as Easy, Moderate, or Challenging. This difficulty rating includes technical skills required to complete the recipe as well as time involved. In some recipes, the skills are easy, but the time is lengthy, so don't give up on a recipe based on the designation alone. Most recipes in this book are intentionally very easy to complete, but often times take some additional planning time.

SEASON — SPRING — SUMMER — FALL — WINTER — YEAR-ROUND

SOURCE — FOREST — FIELD — FARM

DIFFICULTY — EASY — MODERATE — CHALLENGING

SERVES — 12

"Foraging for food should have the same slogan as kinky sex:
Keep it safe, sane, and consensual." —CHEF ROB CONNOLEY

I wish everyone had been brought up in a home that cooked food from scratch—a home that celebrated food at every family gathering. While my family had its Old El Paso taco nights, the fonder memories are of the liver dumplings we made every Thanksgiving that no one liked. In my family, we weren't afraid to cook, nor were we afraid to try something new. Much of my motivation to write this book was to give you, the reader, a guide to easy but exciting foraged cuisine. Don't leave this new style of food to the chefs and survivalists. I want you to jump head first into this cookbook.

My cuisine has been described as modernist foraged, but that's just silly to me. Modernist cuisine often catches the sneer of being foams and spheres, but like most modernist chefs, I have evolved. I mostly avoid hydrocolloids in this book, as I do other modernist techniques. To me, the heart of the modernist movement is capturing amazing natural flavors, presenting them beautifully, and pairing them in ways that may not be expected.

If I ask my prep cooks what to pair with smoked salmon, I might hear dill or wasabi. Both are great pairings, but let's push a bit further. I see maple with smoked salmon, often in the form of a glaze on the fish. But we're not done yet. Maple takes me to corn, chocolate, brown sugar, and cinnamon. Well, that's a Mexican chocolate, isn't it? So why can't we pair a smoked salmon with a dark, rich drinking chocolate? See one of my earliest favorites with the smoked salmon marshmallow with Mexican Drinking Chocolate (page 83), which tantalizes the tongue by balancing the richness of a more savory version of drinking chocolate with the unusual, yet sweet, complement of a gooey marshmallow.

I want you to take risks. My bathroom-inspired celery dessert evolved from sniffing a bar of hotel soap. You wouldn't eat soap, but great successes come from great risks. Risks shouldn't be taken for risk's sake. Risks should be taken to stretch your comfort zones, because by stretching yourself, new discoveries are made. Don't serve my Elk's Blood Bonbons (page 86) to shock your friends. Serve it because it's good. And it's for those reasons that I often don't tell people what they're eating, because I don't want barriers to go up.

When we add the element of foraged ingredients into the mix, we heighten the risk of shock for shock's sake. Be smart with foraged foods. Get solid training. Serve ingredients only when you are absolutely sure they are safe.

In behavioral sciences, *efficacy* refers to that point where knowledge and confidence meet—"flow," in sporting terms. You're in the zone. That's the point you want to reach as a cook or a chef. You should develop a set of skills that you know like the back of your hand so that if I throw you a new ingredient, you can respond without conscious thought. This book is just another tool for you, but use it more as inspiration than as the rulebook. I believe all cookbooks should be treated that way.

I was once served a multi-course dinner at a small unknown restaurant that came line by line from *Alinea*—one of the bibles of the molecular gastronomy movement. The chef had missed the point of a cookbook, and his food reflected that, as it was slightly off and sterile. Please do follow these recipes, whether they be for more complicated dishes, like the Poached Yolks (page 109), or the simple Peanut Butter Pie (page 127), but then make your own creations with this new information.

On a more concrete level, be prepared to adjust times, temperatures, and measurements to meet your kitchen and environment. For example, I live in a very dry climate, so my flour needs much more moisture to hydrate and will weigh less on the scale than if I were in a more humid climate.

Finally, have fun with it. Don't overthink it. Get in the zone, find locally foraged fare, and get cooking!

1 FORAGING, ETHICS &
THE BUILDING
OF A RESTAURANT:
RE-VISIONING THE
FOOD WE EAT

GO LOCAL

Have you ever noticed how you can eat in a dozen restaurants in different parts of the country, and the food all tastes the same? Even in top restaurants, I can taste when the chef is using ingredients from a food-service distributor, following recipes turned into clichés by culinary schools, and plating in the style that everyone sees on culinary websites. This is the homogenization of our food.

When people talk about buying local, they typically are talking about doing it for economic or environmental reasons. But for me, it's about flavor. I don't want my food to taste like food you might get in other restaurants. I want it to be personal, special, and unique. I want it to be a manifestation of my life, my experience, and my surroundings.

As you create the recipes in this book, find the local honey, goat cheese, and meats. They will taste different than mine, and that's a great thing. They'll be fresher, more seasonal, and certainly more uniquely yours. These are the ingredients that will make your meal special.

LOOK UP. LOOK DOWN.

On most foraging walks, I'm either looking up or down. Grapevines (up) or watercress (down). It really is hard to do both if you're foraging in the woods, because even the most barren trails offer so much to see. So on most walks, I am either looking up or looking down, but rarely both. Sometimes, this required concentration can lead to more problems than you might expect.

One of my favorite foraging spots is an old ranch that long ago was sold into a conservation trust. A creek meanders through it almost year-round and is rife with watercress, various bitter greens, cattail, crawfish, and ducks. On one walk, I decided the area must have wild grapes—the environment was perfect for them—even though I had never noticed them before. Instead of heading upstream to my usual foraging area, I headed downstream. Carefully walking on the small cobbles, I looked along each tree branch for distinctive grape leaves or fruit clusters, but saw nothing.

I continued walking, brushing the occasional branch out of my face, still keeping my eyes upward for a new bounty.

I should have known something was wrong when my dog, Lexi, jumped suddenly and dodged away with an alarming yip, but I assumed she had stepped on a cactus or was bitten by a bug. Before I could see what spooked her, a sulfurous stench hit my nose, sending my hackles up just as quickly. I looked down and, sure enough, just one long step away, a full-grown skunk was turning her hind end around to spray. I bolted, but too late to escape unscathed. On that day, Lexi and I suffered for our art. My ritual of visiting the diners was broken for the next few nights, recusing myself to the kitchen with its strong exhaust fans.

As you begin your foraging journey, be sure to take in all of your surroundings, the ground beneath your feet, and the sky above your head. You may thank me for it later.

TIMING

Timing is everything with foraging. Every plant and ingredient has a season. Some of the most time-sensitive ones include green walnuts and cattail pollen. Both ingredients have a harvesting window of less than two weeks, but for each, the prime picking is actually marked in just days.

The first year I harvested cattail pollen, I had been watching my stand, waiting for the final male baton to shoot up past its furry female bulb. As a few broke through their papery sheathes, I noted that I needed to come back very soon to harvest the larger expanse of the stand. Two days later, I returned, jar in hand, only to find the majority of plants had already shot up and released their pollen load. As I went along, plant by plant, lightly flicking the batons to check the pollen amounts, I found that all but a few had dried up and were being consumed by various insects. It was a season lost—fifty weeks of waiting, and I missed it by a day!

Foraging requires diligence and patience to maximize the harvest. In my most recent cattail pollen–gathering season, once I observed the first baton as it revealed itself, I started returning to that spot every morning and night for the next ten days. The result was a sustainably harvested quart of pollen, more than enough for my intended uses and plenty for some experimenting to boot. Mother Nature's pace can be both slow as a snail and fast as a sparrow.

If you nurture your favorite foraging spots, you'll learn their personalities; their pace, and their reactions to rain, to dryness, heat, cold, your path trampling, your dogs' knocking them down, and much more. Become in tune with your food, and your timing will sharpen and produce better results.

FOOTPRINTS IN THE SAND

You've seen the posters and read the sappy poem. "Footprints in the Sand" is always accompanied by a picture of a beach at sunset. The poem is a beautiful sentiment of heartwarming words. But when I see footprints in the sand where I forage, I think, "Uh oh. I hope they're just hiking through and not picking the mint."

It's not a matter of greed—rather, it's more a matter of stewardship.

When I first began my foraging life, I bought a number of topographical maps of the area and studied them for springs, creek beds, and steep crags that might funnel into a predictable gathering space. These make obvious spots for plants to grow—especially in the arid desert Southwest. I wanted locations that were not readily accessible to wandering tourists, but accessible enough for an avid hiker like myself. If a road was near the water source, I wasn't interested.

If a trail approached the water source, I looked at how hiker-friendly it was. In the end, I found a small handful of spots where I didn't expect to ever see other humans, and where there would be no obvious risk of contamination from cars, mines, or questionable water runoff.

These spots I first discovered are ones that I have nurtured for years. I take care not to damage the environment by trampling plants, breaking branches, or overharvesting. I have come to know my trails very well, and the plants there have become old friends.

So when I see footprints, I get nervous. Are they harvesting, or just passing through? Are they going to step on that new sapling that shot up last week, or will they step over it? I hope they don't step on the rock the big crawfish lives under because I've been watching to see how big he'll actually get to be.

I am sentimental about my favorite foraging areas. And that's why I fear the footprints in the sand.

FORAGING ETHICS

While there are no hard and fast rules for foraging, we should all learn from the experience of those who have gathered before us. The following guidelines were shared with me by my mentors. Most of them were influenced by the Apaches in the area, and all should be considered launching-off points, not the final word. Your local foragers will welcome the opportunity to share issues relevant to the woods and fields in your area . . . you just need to ask.

BASIC GUIDELINES

1. Forage only in established groves/ stands/plants

Since I forage in the vast wilderness, and almost always off-trail, I often stumble upon great new ingredients, whether it be my recent find of wild plum or a lonely saltbush. And before I start plucking and cutting, I have to decide whether the plant can sustain my harvesting. It is always tempting to just rape and pillage, but that's a short-term approach that leads to scarcity and the loss of future ingredients. Determine the vitality of the plant, the amount of water the plant has been getting, and how much the plant will offer you. The goal of the forager is to manage the plant so it grows stronger and more beautiful each year. Trim carefully with next year in mind.

2. Consider what roles the plant may play in the diets of area wildlife

I am constantly pondering the *Star Trek* prime directive, which prohibits Starfleet personnel from interfering with the internal development of alien civilizations. And so it should be here. Assume that animals are all around and watching you steal their food. Don't make them angry, and better yet, don't let them know you were even there after you've gone. That doesn't mean that you should hesitate to forage; just do so with an awareness of the larger ecosystem.

3. Do no harm when approaching the foraging area

Every Boy Scout knows that you leave only footsteps and take only photos when you hike, but foragers are going to be bringing back more than photos—if they're lucky, they'll be bringing back a big basket of fresh mushrooms! Your job is to gather. It is not to break branches, knock down dead trees, or weed-whack tall grasses to make your path easier. If you find yourself clearing a path because it is too overgrown, or knocking down a beehive because you can't gather your oyster mushrooms, then you shouldn't be foraging that day. You are a visitor to the land, not the lord of it.

4. Do not pick anything within sight of a road or other area of pollution or contaminated runoff

Of all my ethical guidelines, this is the most ambiguous. I choose not to gather anything in sight of, or downhill from, any source of pollutant—especially roads. I have that luxury living in the wilderness. I haven't been able to do soil and toxicological testing on what I consider risky foods, so I choose to simply steer clear. I tell other chefs: if you're willing to tell your customers where you gathered the food, and willing to eat it yourself, then go right ahead. If you have any hesitation with either of those ideas, then don't pick risky foods.

WORTHWHILENESS GUIDELINES

Once you've established that you can ethically and sustainably harvest ingredients, consider whether you should. It's not just "Can I?" but also "Should I?" Here is how I determine if I should:

1. Must taste great

My foraging mentor wants me to love many tree barks and bitter greens, but I just can't get into them. I prefer the sweetness of the hackberry or the tangy burst of juice from the currant. Taste. Judge. Decide if it will be part of your next meal.

2. Must digest well

Literally, will your body digest this ingredient? Will your stomach ache because it has too much fiber or because the bitterness is too intense? Start easy and develop a body that accepts foraged food well. Learn how to properly cook bitter greens and juicy berries. As a chef, I need to prepare foods for guests who will eat popotillo just once in their lives, so I need to do it in a way that is pleasurable as it digests.

3. Must give your body good energy

When I eat wild oyster mushrooms, my body simply feels good. When I eat factory-raised pork, my body does not. Every food interacts with your body differently and results in a certain energy. This isn't wahoo hippie talk, but instead a physiologic response. Be attentive to the response; nurture what your body likes, and minimize or avoid what it doesn't.

4. Must be abundant

I will beat this drum repeatedly—don't eat anything at the expense of the plant you are foraging. If there is only one wild rose bush, and it's producing minimally, then leave it alone.

5. Must be easy to harvest

Think bang for the buck. We are currently working on grass seed as a food source in the kitchen (see Richard Felger, p. 140), and the potential is huge from a macro-agricultural perspective. But oy, the work involved—hours upon hours to gather enough grass to yield just a cup. Grass's future in my kitchen is yet to be determined, although I think you'll enjoy my Wild Grass Risotto (p. 143). On the other hand, hackberry is even more challenging to gather than grass seed, but the flavor payout is huge and well worth the time invested.

6. Must be easy to prepare

I avoid many of the bitter greens because they often take multiple boils or steams to get them palatable for the restaurant's clientele, but horehound needs only a simple steeping. Each plant will require a certain amount of labor, and you will determine the value to your diet.

A TIP FOR CHEFS:
Building a Foraging Team

If you're foraging for yourself, you can head out the door with a basket and gloves. But if you're looking to forage for a restaurant, you need to do more due diligence. Just as in a restaurant kitchen, where your team members have areas of expertise—you have your fish guy, your salad boy, your steak girl—in a foraged-foods kitchen, you need experts. Even with stacks of field guides and a web browser full of tabs, it is impossible for one person to have enough knowledge to serve customers amazing, safe food night after night if the kitchen is going to make full use of the land.

Early in my career, my greatest concern was determining which plants were edible. I consulted local hippies, mountain men, and vocal vegetarians. One afternoon I was talked about popotillo to an herbalist friend and mentioned how I had served it to customers. She shared her concern that popotillo contains a form of ephedra. She has since told me about common plants that can elevate blood pressure, thin blood, cause light-headedness, and even activate menstrual cycles. This key member of my team now serves as my health expert and devil's advocate.

Armed with the information she had shared with me, I then sought out an old friend who travels the mountains, dragging his burro along while looking the part of a hillbilly leprechaun. He is known in the region for his spiritual connection to the land, his ability to survive on the mountain harvest, and his deep understanding of what historic and prehistoric peoples ate.

Our local university provides me with biologists, botanists, artists, and historians who give me an academic perspective of our wilderness and who can engage me in conversations about ecology, sustainability, and foraging ethics. My academic team members' synergies continue to grow. Recently, I have been working with a professor who is interested in indigenous grasses as a sustainable food source. He knows which grasses are best for foods and how they have historically been consumed, but relies on me to find modern ways to winnow and prepare the seeds so others can view grass as a food source.

My final team members are Forest Service and Bureau of Land Management (BLM) professionals, with whom I am in constant contact. They help me stay legal in my gathering, and these friends in adult Boy Scout uniforms also steer me toward very interesting things. My first interaction with Forest Service staff was when one told me about the over-abundance of crawfish in the Gila River. I asked if I needed a permit to gather them and was told to take my fill: crawfish are an invasive species the Forest Service is trying to eradicate because they consume food that should instead go to the native fish that they are re-introducing.

Forest Service staff have also become my eyes and ears. Our Gila Wilderness is vast, and often they'll tell me about a stash of morels or a herd of javelinas deep in the woods. Because of our ongoing relationship, they know I harvest sustainably, and they trust me with information that normally wouldn't leave their office walls.

Whether for reasons of safety, or simply to get location tips, there is more information that you need to know than you can ever find by yourself. A foraging team addresses one of the biggest concerns of a foraged-food restaurant, and that is government oversight. In most states, restaurant codes direct that food must come from "approved sources." But what is an approved source for lichen or monkey flower? By developing a team of experts, fastidiously documenting your diligence around ensuring food safety, and ultimately preparing the foods in an inspected kitchen, you become the approved source for your foraged-food kitchen. For the home cook, your foraging team is the perfect group to share your meal with while exchanging stories and hidden treasures.

LEXINGTON ELIZABETH:
Master Forager

Lexi entered my life when she was just five days old. We lived across the street from a woman who worked at a veterinary clinic, and one day she told us about a litter that had been rescued from a hunter who wanted the puppies destroyed. When we walked into the clinic and saw the staff nursing little white fluffballs with closed eyes, it was love at first sight. As Lexi's eyes opened, there I was, as imprinted on her as she was on me.

Lexi is a mix of blue tick hound and blue heeler—amazingly smart and fiercely loyal. Her snow-white pelt dotted with black dots gives the appearance of blue-gray. She has a docked tail and lush eyelashes. She quickly became my baby and best hiking bud. Years before the restaurant was a dream or foraging the goal, Lexi and I scoured the remote and rugged mountains in the Gila Wilderness together. She never moves farther than twenty feet from me until a rabbit or deer comes into sight; then, she is gone, leaving me to hear the ever-fainter *yap, yap, yap!* as she heads off into the mountains. Whether I keep walking or stay put for five minutes or a half hour, she always rejoins the trail right where I am—more accurate than any GPS I've ever owned.

She always needs work to occupy her mind. We'd trained her to recognize thirty words and ten or so tricks, and when we started foraging together, it was time for more work lessons, which she happily accepted. Our first job was with juniper berries, by happenstance. I rate all junipers by two factors—sweetness and astringence. For example, my current batch is rated 4-7, meaning mid-sweet/a bit on the not-sweet side (4), and fairly strong astringency (7). One day while I was picking, Lexi started wolfing down the berries. I moved to another bush that wasn't as good, and she didn't eat those berries. And so I started formally training her by carrying a bag of dog treats and rewarding her by giving her a dog treat each time she ate a berry that I liked. When I found berries I didn't like, I would feed them to her and not offer a treat. It took just days for her to figure out her job—easy work with a good payout!

Likewise, I trained Lexi to forage acorns. Unlike juniper berries, which I find are always usable, acorns are either good or bad—there is no in-between. I took Lexi to one of my favorite hikes in the Black Range, a place that's littered with acorns that crunch under every step for miles. Using the same training technique, I would treat Lexi each time she ate a good acorn, and not treat her when she ate a bad acorn. Lexi picked up the job within an hour and filled my pantry with good acorns that were tasty and required almost no processing. And so it has been with morels, horehound, and a variety of other plants.

I hope you can take a special someone along on your foraging hikes. Maybe it will be your daughter. Maybe it will be your neighbor. And if you're really lucky, it might be your favorite four-legged friend.

GATHERING INGREDIENTS

I want you to get out and forage. Leave your kitchen. Get off of your desk chair. Go outside and eat. Despite the warnings and rules and ethics statements in the previous pages (all done to make you the best forager you can be), foraging does not have to be scary, and eating food from the land should not be relegated to the "experts."

This book purposefully focuses on plants and animals you can find throughout most of North America. Even some of the cactus ingredients are found in the northern states. I gave my mother in St. Louis a cactus over a decade ago, and today it's plump and continues to bear fruit in its original pot in her window.

Yes, please use caution. Absolutely be ethical in how you gather. But do forage. Start by Googling "What plants in my state will kill me?" That's a good starting point, right? Follow my advice in the previous sections and then go. Decide what your tolerance is for pollution. Remember that organic farms are located in populated areas that get the same water and air as many forageable parks. Decide for yourself. Either way, it's safer than grocery-store fruits and vegetables, which are sprayed with pesticides, fungicides, or herbicides.

The advice that follows is not intended to be comprehensive. There are plenty of great books for detailed plant identification (see *Resources*). This advice will tell you when and how to harvest to get the best flavor and allow the plants to sustain for future foraging. Just go already!

ACORN

To gather your own, ideally look for gray or Emory oak trees. Scout them out early in the year, because when you get to late September or early October, you'll be in a race against the squirrels. If you're really organized, lay a skirt of sheets around the trees so when the acorns fall, you can gather them easily and take the nuts back to your house for shelling. If acorns sit on the ground for too long, they can get worms. Worms aren't the worst things in the world, but many gag at the thought of eating them.

In regard to sustainability, you'll never be able to gather all the acorns that fall, so you'll leave plenty for future propagation and plenty to share with the squirrels, no matter how loudly the little beasts scream at you while you search the forests.

To process acorns, pop the caps off and save them for meat smoking or garden mulch. Sort through the nuts and remove any with wormholes. Crack the shells of those that remain either with the heel of your hand or a hammer. Remove the shells (a tedious job) and place the nuts in a colander. (I like to use a colander because I like to shake out the acorns to remove small shell fragments when finished.)

Next, eat the acorn to determine its quality. How bitter or astringent is it? If it's sweet and nutty, store the nuts in a cool, dry environment or freeze them in an airtight container. If the acorns have a tannic quality, you need to remove that bitterness. Traditionally, acorns are leached in water, but I prefer to remove the tannins through dehydration. Dry the nuts for a minimum of three hours either in a dehydrator or in an oven at the lowest setting with the door kept cracked open with a wooden spoon. Taste the acorns again and continue dehydrating if tannins are still present.

Since I use them primarily for flour and starch, I then coarsely grind the acorns in the food processor and dehydrate the ground acorns for another hour.

Finally, I transfer them to a blade coffee grinder and turn acorn meal into my acorn flour. Seal the flour in an airtight container and store in the freezer.

Every tree grows different acorns based on the type of oak and the terroir. If this drying method doesn't work for your specific acorns, try the more traditional water-leaching process, which you can find on any homesteading website. If at the end of the day you can't forage edible acorns, buy acorn starch at a Korean market or online (see *Resources*). I've found that using the starch works well with baked goods and provides a bit of crunchiness to some recipes. However, the starch can only be used in batters and puddings, because of its fine texture. For dishes like the Acorn Croquettes with Baked Cashews (p. 154), you need a crunchier nut, so if you can't forage edible acorns, you need to substitute a different nut, like pecans.

AMARANTH

Amaranth should be gathered in the window between when it has gone to seed but before the winter winds release the seeds to the ground. The seeds are smaller than poppy seeds.

You can certainly enjoy amaranth baby greens in late winter and early spring (while avoiding frost-damaged plants, as they may be toxic), but my preference is for the seeds, which have a somewhat oily texture and a strong, nutty flavor.

With a bare hand, grab the seed stalk at its lowest point. With your free hand, hold a small bucket or bag just below the stalk. Firmly pull upward on the stalk, stripping the seed pods from the stalk and allowing them to fall into the bucket or bag. I recommend using your bare hands because you need to be able to feel whether you should squeeze harder or relax the pressure to maximize the harvest. Because these plants are such prolific seeders, you will be able to fill a five-gallon bucket in less than a half an hour. A five-gallon bucket will net about two cups of seeds after winnowing.

Amaranth is a weed. Gather as much as you want. It likes to grow along roads, but you can find more pristine plants along country dirt roads that don't get much traffic pollution.

Winnowing is the process of removing the husk from the seed, or in this case, helping the tiny seed fall

out of the husk. Start by putting a tight-fitting lid on your bucket or tying your bag closed. Shake the container aggressively, and then violently. Use the shaking to work out your childhood traumas! Besides feeling better about your life, you will release 75 percent of the seeds. Next, open the container and rub the husks between the palms of your hands. Again, be aggressive—you are trying to free a captive seed. Do this until all the husks have been rubbed.

Next, I like to transfer all of the husks and seeds to a large, rectangular, plastic bin of the type used for storing holiday decorations and clothes. Go through the husks one more time, rubbing them between your palms. This whole process should take a half an hour for a five-gallon bucket. Move the bin outside—not on a blustery day—and fan the bin with a magazine to blow out the empty husks. Don't be so aggressive that you lose your hard-earned seeds, but enough that the husks blow out of the bin. You should see a generous layer of tiny, shiny, black or brown seeds on the bottom. Continue, increasing your fanning force, until all that is left are the seeds and a little dust. Transfer the seeds to your finest mesh strainer and strain out the dust. Any remaining dust will be considered "dietary fiber." Store the seeds in an airtight container in the refrigerator for up to six months.

CATTAIL

Cattails are the plants I forage more than any other. It is also the plant I am most careful with, for safety and propagation. You will find cattails along marshy roadways, but you don't want those plants. Look for hidden marshes and ponds instead. You will be able to harvest different parts of the plants at different times of the year.

Spring shoots are delicious—juicy, flavorful, and tender. About a month after the last frost, shoots will start popping up. Using a knife, cut the shoots just below the water level in a clean, decisive cut, leaving the roots intact. If you cut this way the plant will send out a new shoot within just a couple weeks. To enjoy the shoots, peel off the woody outer layers, trim the tops, and eat! The shoots are reminiscent of cucumber. Take no more than a quarter of the plants during this early spring harvest.

Allow the plants grow. They grow quickly. I like to watch my groves weekly throughout April and May to measure the growth. Near the end of May, a small pointy end will grow out of the top of the tall, grass-like stalk. This end will then grow a tight green mass shaped like a small hot dog. I don't serve this part, which becomes the flower head, but if you do, keep your harvesting to a minimum, because the gold is still to come. You can sauté the flower head and eat it like corn on the cob.

Once the flower has developed, you should watch the grove daily, if possible. The flower head will send up a pointy stick. That pointy stick will be covered in a yellow powder—the pollen, the gold! The window of opportunity to gather pollen is very small. If it rains or the wind blows, you can lose all the pollen until next year. At best, you will have two weeks to gather the pollen, but recognize that the longer the pollen is on the plants, the more likely you are to have to battle bugs in it.

If you are in an area with concentrations of indigenous people, check to see if they gather pollen for ceremonial purposes in your area, and if they do, be respectful.

It is important that you not overharvest the pollen so the plant can grow and bugs can gather pollen as well. To gather, carry a tall, clean jar in one hand, and, using your other hand, bow the stalk down, allowing the pollen tip to get inside the jar but not so far as to break the stalk. Give the tip a flick against the inside top of the jar. Carefully remove the plant from the jar opening. If you gather early in the window, each flick will yield about one tablespoon per plant. You can fill a pint-sized jar in about thirty minutes.

The pollen makes for a nice garnish and has a dirty-sweet, almost citrusy flavor that works well in a number of recipes.

ROB CONNOLEY: GATHERING MINT

HACKBERRY

As you'll find in the recipes section, I love hackberries. With their concentrated, date-like flavor, hackberries are relatively easy to gather, are plentiful, and require almost no processing.

Around mid-October, the berries will start to dry on the tree. I've yet to find a good use for the berries before they dry, and the lack of birds eating them suggests that they don't have much purpose throughout the summer. Depending on the voraciousness of your local birds, you can find the dried berries all the way into January, although in much scarcer quantities than in late October.

To harvest, use one hand to hold a bag or jar with a large mouth and pluck the berries with your other hand, one at a time. You'll be tempted to strip the branch as you do with amaranth, but with hackberry, you want to make sure that you don't damage the tree. So be patient. Enter your Zen space. And pluck. One. By. One. You'll give up after an hour with only a cup or two to show for your efforts, but that's enough for most recipes. Because of the bounty of hackberries, you can come back to the same spot next weekend, when you're tired of the baby crying or the dog barking, and pluck in peace, solitude, and silence. While the seed is edible if it's ground, I prefer to use hackberry to steep flavor.

MESQUITE

Mesquite is available June through September, and the plants will often go through two flowering cycles in that time. There is a slight, but real, risk with mesquite in that the pods can gather a bacteria that is toxic. If you see a hole on a pod, move on. Pods on the ground will be more prone to the bacteria and pests, so *only* harvest directly from the tree and never from the ground.

To gather, start by tasting a pod. If it's sweet and enjoyable, continue gathering. If not, move to the next tree. The pods should pull off the branch easily when ripe. Once you've gathered enough, give them a quick dunk in cool water and then spread the pods in a sunny, dry area for a couple of days. Watch for wind and rodents, both of which will make your harvest a bit smaller.

When you're ready to use the mesquite, break the pods into smaller pieces and carefully grind in your food processor or blender. I have my best success using a food processor, but the more common technique is using a blender. Either way, grind and then sift through a mesh strainer, returning the larger pieces to the processor until all of the pod has been ground into a fine powder. Store in an airtight container in the freezer. The pods can also be left whole and steeped into teas or made into syrups. *Eat Mesquite! A Cookbook* by Desert Harvesters is a great primer on mesquite use.

I have yet to encounter a mesquite tree I couldn't harvest to my heart's content, but be aware that animals, including domestic animals like cows, eat the pods as well.

PRICKLY PEAR

You'll learn quickly that not all prickly pears are created equal. For this book, we are only referring to the bulbous magenta fruit, often referred to as "tuna," that shoots off the rim of the green cactus pads. The tuna contains meat that transitions from green and tart to purple and sweet. Both stages are tasty in their own way, but the recipes in this book use the ripened, sweet juice.

You may find tunas in your local Hispanic grocery and many larger grocery stores, where they can be four or five inches long. In my area, they tend to be closer to two inches long. While they are best from June through October, tunas can often be found into the winter. The longer tunas stay on the plant after their ripening peak, the less enjoyable they are. Chefs will often buy prickly pear juice from a distributor, including Perfect Purée out of Napa. Prepacked juice provides consistency but loses the flavor spikes, which I enjoy, of mellow earthiness and high citrus notes.

To harvest, use kitchen tongs to snap tunas from the paddles and carefully drop them into a pillowcase. I rough up my pillowcase by swinging it around and tossing it on the ground. This makes me look a bit nuts to passersby, but it pulls off the majority of needles. Many like to throw the tunas on coals or torch them with blowtorches to burn off the spines, but I find that heat negatively affects the flavor. I then roll out the tunas onto a flat surface and allow the wind to clean the tunas of their spines. The grocery store tunas will already be free of spines.

When you're ready to use the tunas, put the fruit in a large stockpot, whole, and attack them with a potato masher. Smash and mash until a big, slimy mass forms. If the tunas are dry, add a cup or two of water and mash a bit more. Pour the mash into a cheesecloth-lined sieve or dump it into a clean pillowcase suspended above a bowl and let the juice drip into the bowl. Don't force the mash, or you'll end up with slimy juice; just let it drip overnight. You can either use it immediately or freeze the juice for later. If your sole purpose is margaritas (which is a very good sole purpose), then freeze the juice in ice-cube trays.

Gathering the fruit does not affect the health of the plant if you are careful to snap the fruit and not break off the paddle. That said, be conscious of animals in the area that might survive on the fruit. If there's only one plant around, leave it for the deer or javelinas. If you have plenty of prickly pears, gather no more than half the tunas from any one cactus.

SPRUCE TIPS

Spruce tips appear at the very earliest sign of spring. There are about a half-dozen common North American spruce species north of Mexico, both wild and cultivated. The tips are the obvious new growth on the ends of the branches, with needles that are yellow-green instead of the older dark green. Simply snip them with shears. A mature spruce will put off up to one hundred new tips, and removing the tips actually promotes a healthier plant. Allow yourself to remove no more than half—just snip every other branch. To control awkward growth that could damage the tree, don't overharvest easy-to-reach spots.

Rinse well in cold water and let soak for thirty minutes in a bowl of water with 1 tablespoon of Dawn dish detergent for every quart of water. Rinse extremely well again and store on a paper towel in a sealed container in the refrigerator for up to a week.

SUMAC

In my area, sumac is commonly called the lemonade plant for a good reason—the fruit tastes like lemons. In almost all instances, you steep the dried fruit in a liquid and strain it out to tease the citrus flavor into your recipe. The stalks are very distinctive, coated with orange-burgundy colored fruit. Do not confuse this plant (*Rhus trilobata*) with the common poison sumac found throughout much of the eastern part of North America. I've warned you, so do your homework!

The fruit will start to gain color around late July and will be available for harvest through late August. To gather, snip the berry branches off where the berries begin and carefully set them in a plastic tub. Since you will be steeping the fruit, just keep the branch intact until you're ready to use it. Store the fruit in the refrigerator, or if you want to use sumac later in the winter, hang the branch, tied by a string, to a rod in a dry, sunny location. The flavors will become concentrated. You can use either the fresh or dried fruit for the recipes in this book.

I have not had any problems with overharvesting this plant. Take what you want. Animals don't much like the tart fruit, and when you snip the fruit branch, the sumac will return next year for you to harvest again.

WALNUT

Any walnut tree owner will tell you that as magnificent as its shade is, its fruit is foul and hateful to the ground beneath it. Caustic, astringent, bitter, vile—are just some of the adjectives I hear when I take people foraging with me. But look past the original flavor and see the inner beauty that comes from walnuts with a few years of aging . . . and a liter of vodka (see *Nocino*, p. 183)!

In general, I use Arizona walnuts, but all walnuts can be used in the recipes in this book. There are two gathering periods that we consider. The first is in early to mid-June, when we gather green walnuts from the tree. You want the nuts that are as big and green as they're going to get. Their transition to brown marks their change from soft to hard. You want to pick the nuts when they are the largest while still allowing your knife to cut through them. Many people suggest wearing gloves when gathering walnuts, but I enjoy the smell and discoloration my hands take on after a day of picking. There are online sellers of green walnuts in California, and before I harvested my foraged walnuts, I used to buy from www.MountLassen.com, which picks them at the peak time.

The second gathering period is once the nuts fall to the ground. This happens around mid-September through early October, and you'll be able to find fallen nuts into winter. Gather these nuts and let them sit in a dry area. When they are no longer soft on the outside, smash them with a hammer to reveal the inner meat. You'll quickly learn that there's not much meat, but it is tasty.

Overharvesting is not a problem with walnuts at either time of the year. You won't be able to get the nuts at the top of the tree, and there are more than you'll ever need on any one tree. Gather away and cap off the night with a glass of *nocino* and some aged, hard cheese.

YUCCA

Be careful when harvesting from yucca plants, both so you don't get pricked by the plant and so you don't kill the yucca by pulling the plant from its root. Yuccas have some of the most aggressive and unforgiving needles in all of the wilderness. The tip of its rigid leaf has an ultrasharp point that can easily impale your leg and break off, which could lead to a terrible infection.

In this book, we are only concerned with the succulent, tender, dangling blossoms, which are available in May and June. You should harvest as early as possible, because once their sweet scent is released, the flowers will be filled with bugs. Once the bugs have moved in, you can still use the flowers, but only with more cleaning.

To gather, grab the flower at its base—the point where the petals hit the branch—and pull the flower off, whole, and drop it into a bag. Take no more than a quarter of the flowers on any given plant and remove those flowers from different branches. Bugs are important to our environment and they love these flowers, so share.

Once you gather the flowers, the clock starts ticking, as the petals will soon wilt and go bad. Store the petals on a tray lined with paper towels in the refrigerator for up to three days. When you are ready to use them, fill a large bowl with cold water, add the petals, and swish them around with your hands to dislodge any bugs or dirt. Each petal must then be plucked from the flower base, one by one. Discard the base into your compost. Lay the plucked petals on paper towels again, allowing them to dry and allowing you to do a final inspection for bugs. There are lots of nooks and crannies with yucca blossoms, so you need to really scrutinize them for critters.

The petals of the yucca can be tossed in salads, but I like them best in sweet jams (think rose jam), which complement the desert citrus flavor of the petals. All varieties of yuccas can be eaten in a cooked state.

PROFILE: DOUG SIMONS:
Foraging Instructor

by Andrea Feucht

I didn't mean to see the best foraging expert of the Gila Wilderness in the buff—it just kind of happened that way. Doug Simons had just finished a dip in the Gila River, taking the edge off the afternoon desert sun, when I strolled down his road a few minutes early for what was to be several hours of discussion about plants, nutrition, and sustainability. But first, we had to meet his donkeys.

Unshod in callus-protected bare feet and wearing cargo shorts and a cotton T-shirt—not the snark-worthy loincloth one might associate with someone who lived off the land for nearly two decades—Doug led me over to the fence of the donkeys' area. They've grown nearly as big as horses, this mama and son, and clearly they are accustomed to Doug's personality and voice, trusting him completely. "Trust in Doug" is a theme I would get to know well in the next few hours. It is a trust that is shared by many humans in his life, for his body of knowledge is vast and his passion for our plant world is unrivaled. Over a span of years as his student, Rob learned key parts of Doug's knowledge. In this way, Doug was instrumental in helping Rob find his true voice as a chef while embracing the use of native wild plants.

At the end of his adolescence, Doug decided he was going to make a life communing with the plant world; after acquiring some basic knowledge of survival and edibles, he began living completely off the land. It was an effort to prove to himself that he could succeed, physically just as much as mentally. Knowing that his next meal was up to him was daunting, but within Doug's abilities, so he persevered through fear and occasional hunger. Doug didn't abandon that challenging life for a moment. At the end of a decade, however, he decided that he needed to teach and began an institute to share his knowledge. He went back to the land for another decade, finally spending the most recent ten years in a balance of lifestyles—gathering food and medicinals from nature, as always, but living in a permanent shelter and traveling to teach.

I came to speak with Doug at his home down a washed-out sandy road at the edge of the Gila Wilderness; the home is both functional and minimalist. The home invites outdoor living, with an expansive covered patio that doubles as a cooking space, featuring a countertop dotted with drinking glasses and a few cooking vessels. There's a broken-in straw hat

that looks like it has had many years of noggin protecting hanging on a nail. It looks like the one currently on Doug's head. "Don't pick up that hat," Doug says, motioning to the post, "there's a bird nesting inside."

"You see, they talk to me," Doug says, speaking of the plants. Metaphorically, it's a comforting thought, but he's not talking about abstracts here. Much of his ability sprouts from the real relationship and conversations he has with the plants that supply him—and us—with nourishment and life. Though most of us don't think that we can communicate directly with plants, it's entirely normal to hear about people having conversations with their pets or with some of the higher-level mammals, like dolphins or primates. Doug extends that relationship and that respect to all living things. He is equally thankful and humbled to accept and eat the stalk of a plant as the flesh of an animal.

In terms of sustainability, it makes sense to consider plants as more than mere ingredients for a dish or means to an end. If a forager like Rob or Doug considers his interaction with plants to be a long-term relationship, the conversation changes from "How can I get what I need?" to "How can this relationship be healthy and grow in the long term?"

"Rob wanted to know about wild foods, plain and simple." This is how Doug and Rob came together as builders of knowledge. Rob wanted to be able to bring local ingredients into his cooking, and he wanted to do it right from all angles—sustainability, seasonality, wisdom, and care. Doug was already teaching and sharing his skills, but his workshops were still rare in southern New Mexico. Rob helped change that—bringing students to Doug and creating excitement that there's much more out there in "our own" woods than just a few berries once a year.

Once Rob learned the basics of plant identification and had some practice finding good ingredients and managing his harvest, he was able to move forward and begin using his knowledge. After their first encounter and initial instruction, several years went by as Rob honed his approach to native ingredients. Then, one day in the summer of 2014, Doug walked in the door of the Curious Kumquat and sat down. Rob faced a moment he wasn't even sure would happen—his greatest influence was now going to pay him to dine on foods Rob pulled from nearby based on Doug's knowledge. Rob didn't know whether to be terrified, excited, or reverential—so he chose all three.

As it turned out, Doug was humbled by the reverence that Rob paid to his ingredients. Rob's creativity was something Doug could hardly imagine when he gathered food, but despite the unfamiliarity, everything tasted wonderful. In a sense, this was Rob teaching Doug what it means to take excellent parts and make a greater sum. Rob's food just feels right, and Doug Simons is the man who helped build the foundation on which familiar-yet-challenging dishes like cattail hummus thrive.

According to Doug, "No culture survives on bad food; the cultures either change, or they disappear." This is where real, locally sourced foods show their value—in the health of the people that consume them and the ceremonies inherent in food preparation and consumption. Rituals like dining and sharing foods bridge the gap between our physical and spiritual worlds. Deliberate harvesting of ingredients, careful preparation of foods and flavor combinations, and even the final piece of artwork that is a finished dish on the serving plate—these are examples of ceremony.

FINDING YOUR WAY

My number-one rule when I opened the restaurant was never to cook foods that people can do a better job making themselves at home. Nothing pains me more than going out to eat and having foods that are clearly not as tasty, fresh, or nutritious as what I could prepare myself—and having to pay for them.

Somewhere in my development as a cook, that primary rule led me to find my authentic food voice. If you were to ask me exactly what the voice whispers, or to describe its timbre and phrasing, I'd struggle to answer you. But, I do know when I'm off track. Typically, "off track" starts with using someone else's recipe. But all cooks have to begin somewhere, whether it be the recipe of a loving grandparent or the pages of a cookbook.

I believe that young chefs and home cooks should avoid thinking about their voice until they've been in the kitchen for many years. While I've cooked for as long as I can remember, I began to get serious when I baked my way through Pierre Hermé's early pastry books, which he co-authored with Dorie Greenspan. I slavishly followed the rules, learning the techniques, copying the plating. Those books launched other books by Ann Ammernick, David Lebovitz, and many others.

Then something clicked. All of a sudden I recognized patterns—similar techniques, similar ingredients, and familiar plating. My abilities and confidence rose. You can't force that to happen. It just does.

That makes you confident and competent, but not a chef with a clear voice.

The uniqueness happens when you put the books away, and cook foods that excite you, using ingredients that interest you, and share them in a way that has you looking out the kitchen window to see how the guests like their food. That doesn't come from rote execution, but rather from playful enthusiasm. After my years in the kitchen, I still ask my servers what every customer says about every dish, and with some dishes I still sneak out to hear the response from the crowd. I want to hear the giggles, the mmms, and the gasps. If I didn't, there would be no point in my being in the kitchen. Last, I never cook food that I don't want to eat: passion comes only from creating food you want in your own mouth.

Your guests should see your personality in your food. For me, they discover a sense of adventure (unexpected ingredients, playful flavor combinations) and a sense of humor. I find food and our relationship to it funny. I used to dust my goat cheese with cattail pollen expressly because yellow mold on cheese is dangerous and the pollen made the cheese look ruined—when in fact it was some of the best aged cheese I've ever had. No one got the humor except me, but daring souls enjoyed a great cheese. And the hallmark of my culinary voice is pure flavors. In an era when chefs love to make ingredient A taste like ingredient B, I prefer to make ingredient A explode in pure A-ness.

My hope for aspiring cooks and chefs is that they find their authentic voices. Make food only you can make. Plate your food in a way that appeals to you, and not how you saw it on Instagram. Be more passionate about your food than anyone else can be. Do these things, and you will stand out. Easier said than done, but these guides will help you find your way. And for the aspiring chef: if you stay true to yourself and don't try to find followers, the followers will find you and be forever loyal.

2 FROM THE FOREST (ANIMALS)

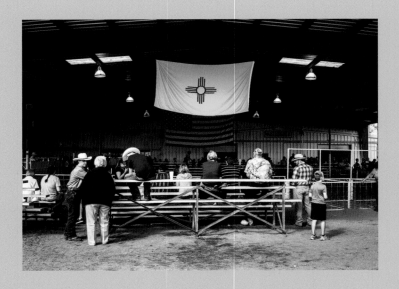

THE MATTER OF MEAT

It's all well and good to be a foraged food restaurant, but customers want a piece of meat on the plate at the height of the meal. The question for us was how to obtain meat in a way that was consistent with our stance on sustainability, ethics, and seasonal freshness. Our restaurant distributors offered "local meats," which were actually meats produced by large ranches many hours, and sometimes states, away. My friends in town who had small numbers of livestock weren't raising at a level that would be able to provision a restaurant.

Our breakthrough happened a number of years ago when a local goat rancher, Becky Campbell, held her annual goat sale. She had a pen of cute, bleating goats of all shapes and colors. Children and their parents gathered around the pen looking for milkers, lawn trimmers, or just cute pets. But I had an eye for a different use. This was the first time in my cooking career that I met my meat. When it was my turn at the corral, I petted a few and settled on a sierra brown-and-white spotted beauty. I told Becky, "This is the one." Off to the truck it went, only to come back to me a couple of weeks later in white paper wrappers.

That goat was for personal use, but it sent me down the path toward our local ranchers, and in particular to the 4-H youth in our community. 4-H (head, heart, hands, and health) is a youth program founded in the early 1900s to develop character and leadership skills primarily though agricultural and government activities. In our remote, rural community, 4-H youth are easy to find, but you can find them in most cities as well.

I followed the 4-Hers to our county fair where these kids duke it out for top goat, pig, or steer. Each year at the fair, my goal is to develop a new meat-buying relationship for the upcoming year. First, I meet with the 4-H adult advisor, who introduces me to some of the kids who have animals that won't become champions (champion animals are very expensive and used more for breeding). Next, I introduce myself to the kids and let them know that I'm in the market to buy meat. It's a tough day for many of these young people, realizing that the animal that they've spent the better part of a year raising will soon be killed and eaten. But it's the business and life on the ranch.

Next I return to the advisor and ask how much the various animals are selling for to the packinghouses. Animals that don't get sold to individuals as winners are most often sold to packinghouses that pay bottom dollar. In a recent year, pork sold to the packer for 50 cents a pound. I then ask the advisor how much the kids have invested in their animals, between buying the animals and their feed. That same year, raising the pigs cost the kids about $1.50 per pound (a potential loss of a dollar a pound). As soon as the competition ends, I approach the children and offer them a fair price. That year, I offered $2 per pound—$1.50 per pound more than the packer and 50 cents more than their investment. Good for the kids' self-esteem, good for the kids' pocketbooks, and a fair price for me.

The animals are sent to a USDA processor to be killed, bled, and skinned, but are returned nearly whole for the kitchen staff to break down into hams, steaks, bacon, roasts, and sausage scraps. We work closely with the processor to separate our animals from the others in order to minimize stress.

Back in the kitchen, we are challenged to be better cooks, knowing the history of our animal demands that we not waste. What we know about javelina backstrap may not translate into cooking pork loin, so each animal pushes us to research, practice, and perfect cooking techniques to pull out the best flavor and texture. It's a rewarding process I encourage you to delve into as well.

This progression from meeting your dinner and looking it in the eye to shopping for your meats from local youths could challenge your commitment to eating local meats. It's hard work, and the relationships that are built, while rewarding, are also heartbreaking when you know that you're going to be killing a child's pet. But we carnivores shouldn't be blind to our food-supply system. What we serve and what comes from the grocery store has a distinct difference in taste and texture. I don't understand why grocery chicken and pork are slimy; my farmed animals are tacky to the touch but are equally moist.

Buying meat locally allows you to have meat that is natural, flavorful, and part of a local economic system that develops young people and provides a better end product. It's not easy for anyone involved, but it is a purer and more responsible system.

PROFILE: THE BRABSONS
and the Bunnies

by Andrea Feucht

Shawn Brabson would likely prefer not to be called a bunny whisperer; perhaps that's a label his kids would accept with a smile. Caitlin and Riley, the kids, are rabbit-show veterans with championships under their belts along with a love of their family business which, of course, is breeding, raising, and selling rabbits for meat. Along with Alisa, Shawn's wife, the family lives and breathes—and eats—all things rabbit.

Both Shawn and Alisa are from southwestern New Mexico and have been living in Buckhorn, thirty minutes from Silver City, for about a decade. Buckhorn is a town of two hundred with one public business—the Brabsons' roadside market. To fill the hours that come with quiet, rural lives, the kids thought showing rabbits for 4-H would be fun—and they knew their mom had been a rabbit breeder for show not so long before.

With an eye toward competition, they decided to see if they could raise rabbits successfully. The project turned into the family story. When the idea hatched in 2010, Shawn had insisted that rabbit raising should become a full-scale business, saying, "If we're gonna do it, let's really do it!" Alisa was on board—the kids, too—and Mogollon Tails Rabbitry was born. It took some research to find the breeds that Alisa had loved to raise in the eighties. The practice of rabbitry had faded in southern New Mexico, so the Brabsons traveled to Texas to get their starter does and bucks.

In less than four years, the rabbitry has grown steadily and the number of breeds raised has increased. At any given time, seventy to eighty rabbits live in their barn and home. Riley and Caitlin offer stiff competition at any fair they enter, typically winning awards. There's also the side market of county and state fairs, where competition is not just for conformity to a breed's characteristics. For all show animals—pigs to sheep to rabbits—an underlying goal is to connect farmers and breeders to customers. For Riley and Caitlin, their rabbits are products: once judged, they are sold for meat, garnering higher prices for better scores. Among those who show rabbits, one of the best results from a fair is a Grand Champion Meat Pen, in which a group of rabbits is sold to a single buyer. The winner takes home a belt buckle for a prize.

Mogollon Tails was humming along when Rob entered the picture not so long ago. The match was perfect: Rob was scouting the county fair and 4-H shows, hoping to find someone selling rabbits for meat. Mogollon Tails was looking for a restaurateur who would be a regular customer for their meat rabbits. Kismet. At first, Shawn says, Rob bought a few, possibly testing recipes and new ideas. Then, the commerce grew. The big weeks count a dozen rabbits—quite a good take for a small restaurant like The Curious Kumquat, and great fun for the Brabsons. The Brabsons and Rob have worked together over the years to identify the best breeds (satin) and age (twelve weeks) for perfect meat, knowledge that fluctuates by season and by recipe.

The connection between Mogollon Tails rabbits and to the tasty Desert Prairie Rabbit (p. 73) at The Curious Kumquat is one of mutual ambition and creativity. Rob and the Brabsons are happily in the business of rabbits.

BACON JAM POP-TARTS

We use bacon jam as a topping on our restaurant's elk burger, but at home I make these pop-tarts into Sunday-morning deliciousness. It's possible you'll never have anything better in your life!

BACON JAM

454 g (1 lb) bacon slices (cure your own for the best results*)

160 g (1 cup) jalapeños, chopped, seeded

320 g (2 cups) onion, chopped

3 garlic cloves, peeled

180 ml (¾ cup) espresso or strong coffee

120 ml (½ cup) apple cider vinegar

100 g (½ cup) brown sugar, packed

120 ml (¼ cup) maple syrup

120 ml (¼ cup) agave nectar

POP-TARTS

365 g (1½ cups + 2 tbsp) unsalted butter, room temperature

85 ml (⅓ cup) milk, room temperature

1 egg yolk, room temperature

1 tsp sugar

1 tsp salt

575 g (4½ cups) all-purpose flour

1 egg, beaten for egg wash

MAKE BACON JAM:

In a Dutch oven or deep cast-iron skillet, cook the bacon until lightly crisp, tossing regularly to brown both sides. Add the jalapeños, onions, and garlic and stir. Add the remaining ingredients and bring to a boil. Reduce the heat to a simmer and cook at least 2 hours uncovered, stopping when the liquids thicken slightly.

Allow to cool slightly, then transfer the jam to a food processor and pulse into a coarse marmalade texture. Take a big spoonful and taste it for quality control purposes. Take a second spoonful in case you made a mistake with the first quality check. And finally, take a third spoonful just to stick it to the man! Let the remaining jam cool to room temperature. Store in a jar for up to two weeks.

*NOTE: There are many recipes for cured bacon, but we prefer the process outlined by Ruhlman and Polcyn in their must-have book, *Charcuterie*. The only change that we make is adding Marash pepper flakes to our cure mix.

MAKE POP-TARTS:

Preheat the oven to 350°F.

In the bowl of a stand mixer, using the paddle attachment, cream the butter. Add the milk and yolk and mix on low speed. The ingredients will resist combining but will eventually come together. In a separate bowl, whisk the sugar, salt, and flour. Add the dry ingredients to the butter and liquids and mix, increasing the mixer speed to medium-low, until the dough just comes together. Don't overmix!

Remove the dough from the bowl and knead for 1 minute on the kitchen counter. Conventional wisdom tells you to chill dough at this stage, but I say hogwash! Divide the dough into roughly two equal portions. Place a Silpat or sheet of parchment paper on the counter with the dough on top. Lay another sheet of parchment paper on top of the dough and roll out the dough to ⅛-inch thickness. Using a ruler and a pizza cutting wheel, cut the dough into 4 × 6-inch rectangles, leaving the dough on the Silpat. Place the Silpat on a baking sheet and put in the freezer while you roll out the second sheet.

Repeat the process with the second portion of dough, being very precise with your 4 × 6-inch cuts. Remove the first baking sheet from the freezer. You should now be able to peel the chilled rectangles off the Silpat. Using the unfrozen dough rectangles as your pop-tart bottoms, spread bacon jam ¼-inch thick, leaving ½-inch borders all around. Brush the borders with egg wash and then place the partially frozen rectangles on top. The time it takes to assemble these tarts warms the chilled dough enough to shape it, but chilling it first allows you to handle the dough without damaging the shape. Seal the borders with your finger or a fork. Using a paring knife, cut a small slash in the center of the top dough to allow steam to escape. Place tarts in the freezer for 10 minutes.

Because the pop-tarts do not spread during baking, you do not have to separate the chilled tarts from each other.

Bake 15 to 20 minutes, or until the pop-tarts are just starting to get color. If you bake darker, the crust will crack and the filling will ooze out. Enjoy with a Sumac Shandy (p. 135).

HACKBERRY RABBIT PÂTÉ: rabbit livers

HACKBERRY RABBIT PÂTÉ

Our customers love rabbit, but serving all of those legs and loins leaves us with a lot of livers. So what to do? pâté, of course. This recipe is sweet enough that I don't mind sitting down and polishing off a bowl with some French bread, and we've even used it as a savory chocolate bonbon filling for special meals.

135 g (1 cup) hackberries, dried on the tree (p. 34)
1 tbsp peppercorns (we prefer tellicherry)
1 tsp salt
454 g (1 lb) rabbit livers
pinch of cayenne pepper
225 g (1 cup) unsalted butter, room temperature
2 tsp dry English mustard
½ tsp nutmeg, freshly grated
40 g (¼ cup) yellow onion, chopped
1 garlic clove, peeled
60 ml (¼ cup) brandy
80 g (½ cup) currants or yellow raisins

Fill a medium-sized stockpot halfway with water and add the hackberries and peppercorns. Bring to a boil, cover, and reduce to a simmer for 30 minutes to infuse the flavors.

Add the salt to the water. Trim the livers to remove any unwanted tissue or hard spots. Place livers in the water and return to a simmer. Cook for 10 minutes or until the livers turn gray, but leave a bit of pink in the center of the thickest spot.

Using tongs, remove the livers and place in a food processor. Add the remaining ingredients (cayenne, butter, mustard, nutmeg, onion, garlic, brandy, and currants/raisins) and process until smooth. I like a little texture in my pâté, so I stop before it becomes silky. Either transfer to a bowl and enjoy, or pipe into molds and let it set up in the fridge before serving in individual portions.

SUGGESTED SUBSTITUTIONS: You can replace hackberries with dried dates by weight. Chicken livers can replace rabbit livers, but the flavor will be stronger.

PORK BELLY POPPERS

This is my go-to dish for potlucks. These are easy to make and have a huge flavor punch. If you like living dangerously, make a sandwich using these with roasted butternut squash spread and green olives.

900 g (2 lb) pork belly, trimmed
110 g (½ cup) sugar
2 tbsp salt
2 tbsp smoked paprika

Preheat the oven to 225ºF.

Cut pork belly into 6-inch squares and place them on a drying rack nestled into a baking pan to allow the grease to drip away. Bake uncovered overnight or at least 8 hours. Cool the pork belly to room temperature, then carefully cut into 1-inch squares.

In a saucepan, sprinkle a third of the sugar on the bottom over medium heat. As the sugar melts, sprinkle another third. When the sugar is liquid, add the final third and continue melting. Now let the liquid sugar caramelize slightly to a nice amber color. Remove the caramel from the heat. Add the salt and smoked paprika and stir thoroughly. Quickly pour the caramel out onto a Silpat and allow to cool until hardened.

Break the caramel into 1-inch pieces and transfer to a food processor. Grind into a fine powder, stopping before the processor heats up the sugar to the point where it starts gunking up along the sides. Sift the caramel powder through a sieve.

Toss the pork belly cubes in the powdered caramel* to coat. Place the coated pork belly on a Silpat-lined baking sheet and place under a broiler just until melted. Remove the sheet and let the caramel harden. Best served with a big mug of local ale!

*NOTE: For a more refined finish, sieve the caramel powder into a 3-inch circular stencil to an even ⅛-inch depth. Remove the template. Place in an oven at 400ºF for 5 minutes or until melted. Remove from the oven and let the disks cool and harden. Place the disk on top of the pork belly and place under a broiler until just melted, as the caramel circle encases the pork belly. Remove from the heat to let the caramel harden. Serve immediately.

LAMB DOLMAS

Wild grapes are prolific across North America, but more often than not the grapes themselves are not palatable. Their leaves, on the other hand, have numerous uses with just a bit of basic preparation. Dried and ground, the leaves make a nice, sour condiment for soups or rices. But let's look to the near east for inspiration in the classic dolma.

PICKLED GRAPE LEAVES
20 grape leaves, stems clipped at leaf
salt
65 ml (¼ cup) lemon juice

LAMB FILLING
135 g (1 cup) quinoa
2 grape leaves, dried
neutral cooking oil, such as canola
227 g (½ lb) ground lamb
salt and pepper, to taste
40 g (¼ cup) raisins
55 g (¼ cup) feta, crumbled
honeycomb, cut into 2-inch long French fry–sized sticks

MAKE PICKLED GRAPE LEAVES:

Bring a medium-sized stockpot filled with heavily salted water to a boil to blanch the leaves. Fill a large bowl with ice water to shock the leaves and preserve the color. The ice water will be used to stop the cooking of the leaves, so make sure it's large enough. Drop the leaves into the boiling water for 45 seconds, and then immediately transfer them into the ice water. Keep the salted water and let it cool to room temperature.

Stack the leaves in groups of four or five and roll each of the stacks into a tube. Place the rolled leaves into a canning jar and, using the salt water that you reserved from blanching them, fill the jar three quarters of the way to the top. Add the lemon juice and store the leaves in your refrigerator until ready to use for up to 1 year.

SUGGESTED SUBSTITUTIONS: Grape leaves are available at all Middle Eastern markets, but also in many major grocery stores in the pickle section.

MAKE LAMB FILLING:

Boil the quinoa and dried grape leaves in lightly salted water (as if it were pasta) for 10 minutes. Drain the quinoa and discard the leaves. Allow to cool to room temperature.

To a large skillet over medium heat, add enough oil to cover the bottom of the pan. When the oil is hot, add the lamb and cook until browned, seasoning with the salt and pepper, breaking up the meat into small pieces. Remove from the heat and let cool until you can handle with your bare hands.

In a bowl, combine the quinoa, lamb, raisins, and feta. Toss gently to combine all of the ingredients.

Unroll one of the pickled grape leaves and fill with a spoonful of the lamb mixture. Add the honeycomb. Roll the sides of the leaf toward the center vein, and then roll the top tip of the leaf toward the stem end. This is the same technique as many people use for close-ended burritos or Chinese eggrolls. You want to roll tight enough that the dolma feels solid, but not so tight that it rips the leaf. Continue until all of your leaves are filled. Enjoy with a crisp white wine out on your porch just before sunset.

CRAWFISH & POTATOES

Inspired by a Cretan recipe for mastiha shrimp, this dish utilizes the plentiful forages of craw-fish and tree sap. This is a fantastic dish for sundowner cocktails at the end of a hot summer day. The pairing of a nice IPA beer with the crawfish is memory-making.

OLIVE OIL PUDDING
240 ml (1 cup) milk
2 egg yolks
73 g (⅓ cup) sugar
3 tbsp cornstarch
1 tsp salt
3 tbsp olive oil

SALT-BAKED BEETS
908 g (2 lb) salt
45 g (½ cup) ground coffee
2 tbsp fennel seed
2 medium-sized beets, whole
    with the tops and bottoms
    removed
olive oil

CLAYED POTATOES
2 large red potatoes, peeled
30 g (¼ cup) kaolin clay powder,
    food grade
1 tbsp cattail ash (p. 191)
1 tbsp water
pinch of salt

TREE SAP CRAWFISH
frying oil
olive oil, enough to cover
    crawfish completely
½ tsp hardened pine or juniper
    tree sap
454 g (1 lb) crawfish, peeled and
    deveined

GARNISH
fresh borage flowers
zest of 1 lemon

MAKE OLIVE OIL PUDDING:

Heat the milk in a saucepan over medium heat. Meanwhile, combine the yolks, sugar, cornstarch, and salt in a mixing bowl and whisk to combine. When the milk comes to a simmer, pour a third of it into the yolk mixture, whisking constantly. Return the hot yolk mixture to the remaining milk and whisk some more. Return to the heat and cook, stirring constantly, until slightly thickened. Remove from the heat and drizzle the olive oil into the pudding while whisking, and continue until homogenous. Transfer the pudding to a squirt bottle or small dish and allow to cool to room temperature.

MAKE SALT-BAKED BEETS:

Preheat the oven to 350°F.

Combine the salt, coffee, and fennel. In an aluminum loaf pan, pour ½-inch of the salt mixture to cover the bottom. Place the beets stem-end down on the mixture. Cover the beets with the remaining salt mixture, ensuring that no beet is showing through the salt. Place in the oven and bake for 75 minutes or until tender when poked with a toothpick. Let cool enough to handle but still warm.

Crack the beets from their salt casing and use a kitchen towel to rub the skin away from the beets, trimming any sticky skin with a paring knife. Cut beets into ¼-inch cubes and store in olive oil.

MAKE CLAYED POTATOES:

Using a melon baller, make a number of potato balls out of the red potatoes. Boil the balls in salted water for 5 minutes and then let rest in the water for an additional 15 minutes. Remove the balls from the water and pat them dry with a paper towel. In a small bowl, whisk the clay powder, ash, water, and salt until smooth. Hold until ready to serve.

MAKE TREE SAP CRAWFISH:

Heat 3 inches of frying oil to 350°F in a large saucepan. In a small bowl suspended in a water bath at 145°F, heat the olive oil and tree sap and allow to steep for 15 minutes. Dip the fried potato balls in the kaolin clay liquid and add to the plate with the crawfish and beets.

Plate the beets and crawfish, garnishing with Beet Soil (p. 198), olive oil pudding, fresh borage and lemon zest. Fry the potato balls in the hot oil for 5 minutes or until lightly browned. Remove from the oil and drain on a paper towel. Dip the fried balls in kaolin clay liquid from the potatoes and plate with the crawfish and beets.

SUGGESTED SUBSTITUTIONS: Crawfish can be replaced by small shrimp. Cattail ash can be substituted with other vegetable ashes (p 191).

CRAWFISH SAMOSA

When I was a child in Missouri, our family had a small cabin in the woods near Ste. Genevieve (the first European settlement west of the Mississippi). I would spend hours walking the creeks and picking up rocks looking for crawfish to take back to the cabin. My mom would graciously use the small crawfish in a meal to let me know my efforts weren't in vain. Now that I have to process these little guys, I know . . . my mom is a saint!

PEPPER SAUCE
2 red bell peppers
2 tbsp olive oil
pinch of salt

SAMOSA FILLING
neutral oil
2 tbsp unsalted butter
40 g (¼ cup) onion, finely chopped
40 g (¼ cup) red bell pepper, finely chopped
40 g (¼ cup) celery, finely chopped
454 g (1 lb) crawfish, shelled, deveined
55 g (¼ cup) goat cheese, crumbled
pinch of cayenne pepper
pinch of salt
zest of 1 lemon
samosa or egg roll wrappers (available in the produce department)

MAKE PEPPER SAUCE:

Cut the tops and bottoms off the peppers, remove the seeds and membranes, and cut a line down the length of each pepper, resulting in one long strip. Place the peppers skin side up on a baking sheet and set in the oven on broil until the skin blackens and blisters. Remove the peppers from the pan and place in a sealed zip top bag to steam for 10 minutes. Remove the peppers from the bag, peel the charred skin away from the meat, and place the meat in a food processor with the olive oil and salt. Process the ingredients into a smooth paste. Hold until ready to serve.

MAKE SAMOSA FILLING:

Heat a high-sided sauce pan of neutral oil to 350°F with 3 inches of the neutral oil.

Heat a skillet coated with the butter to medium high. Add the onion, bell pepper, and celery, and sauté until just starting to soften. Add the crawfish and cook about 3 minutes or until no longer translucent. Remove from the heat. Combine the sautéed vegetables, the crawfish, and the remaining ingredients, except the wrappers, in a bowl and toss to combine. Using the samosa folding instructions on the back of the wrapper package, fill the wrappers with the crawfish mixture. Let rest in the refrigerator for 30 minutes.

Deep fry the crawfish samosas for 3 to 5 minutes, watching for the wrappers to become golden brown. Remove from the oil and drain on a paper towel.

Serve the hot samosas with the red bell pepper sauce and additional lemon zest.

SUGGESTED SUBSTITUTIONS: Small shrimp can replace crawfish.

PEANUT PIGEON

I believe it was the novel *Celestine Prophecy* that suggested there is no randomness to the people you interact with, and often times it's just a matter of persistence and curiosity that will lead you to the higher reason for your meeting. I once had a local customer who had never been to the restaurant in our seven years of operation come in for a birthday dinner. There was nothing notable about him or his wife, and courses came out without any unusual or unexpected responses from them. They were just normal, everyday guests. When it was time for me to deliver dessert, as often happens, we began to talk about who they were and what brought them to the restaurant. After the usual niceties, they mentioned they raised pigeons and asked if I had ever eaten pigeon—STOP. "You raise pigeons here in town!?" The following Sunday I was at their coop at dusk chasing and butchering twenty birds. And the next night, we had the most unique staff meal I've ever served, and now I'll share it with you.

8 pigeons, cleaned
2 tbsp olive oil
160 g (1 cup) onion, chopped
1 tbsp peppercorns, freshly ground
1 tbsp cayenne pepper
145 g (1 cup) raw peanuts, shelled
1000 ml (1 quart) light beer (I prefer a wheat beer)
160 g (1 cup) tomato, chopped
salt, to taste
neutral cooking oil, such as canola

Rest the pigeons on a wire cooling rack and let air dry in your refrigerator overnight. The cooling rack should allow air to flow on all sides of the birds.

Preheat the oven to 325°F.

In a large saucepan coated with olive oil, sauté the onion and then caramelize it to a nice, deep brown. Add the peppercorns and cayenne and continue cooking on low heat, allowing the spices to infuse into the onions for 30 minutes.

While the onions are infusing, place the peanuts into a large glass measuring cup and microwave on high for 60 seconds. Toss the nuts and return to the microwave, now cooking in 30-second intervals, tossing each time, until the nuts are fragrant. Trust your nose. Once you smell the delicious peanut aroma, you need to stop or you'll burn the nuts. Toss them one last time and add the nuts to the onions, stirring to combine. Add the beer and tomato and bring to a soft boil. Transfer the mixture to a blender and blend until smooth. Taste the sauce, and season with the salt. Return the sauce to the saucepan and continue boiling until the sauce is reduced by half.

Heat a large cast-iron skillet over medium-high heat with enough cooking oil to coat the bottom of the skillet. When the oil shimmers but before smoke is let off, add the pigeons, turning to brown on all sides. This will take no more than 1 minute on each side.

When the birds are evenly browned, pour the sauce over them and place the skillet in the oven, uncovered. Bake for 45 minutes, basting the birds every 10 minutes. Serve over rice with additional toasted nuts on top for texture.

SUGGESTED SUBSTITUTION: If you don't have pigeon, look for quail at the gourmet grocery or Asian market. If neither is available, enjoy this recipe with chicken thighs.

TONGUE SALAD

One of the byproducts of buying and processing your own meats is that you have bits and pieces lying around. For an excellent primer on using less-popular cuts of meat, I strongly recommend McLagan's *Odd Bits*. For this recipe, feel free to mix and match the various tongues to take advantage of what you have.

2 lb tongues from beef, pork, lamb, or goat

60 g (½ cup) dried potato leaves (from your garden or available at Asian markets)

4 fresh whole sage leaves (not powdered)

8 dried grape leaves

heavy pinch of salt

bull's blood beet micro-greens

balsamic vinegar

Place the tongues, whole, in a large stockpot and fill with enough water to cover the meat plus 2 inches. Add the leaves and salt. Bring to a boil, reduce to a simmer, and simmer uncovered. Beef and pork will simmer for 3 hours, while lamb and goat will simmer for 2 hours. Add the lamb and goat tongues and continue simmering for 90 more minutes.

Remove tongues from liquid and set aside. Strain the brine. Measure 2 cups of the strained liquid into a saucepan and reduce by half. Reserve and keep warm.

Let the tongues cool just enough to handle them. Peel the skin from the tongues. The skin should peel rather easily with your bare hands. Trim the edges and any unwanted sections. Slice the meat, against the grain, as thin as possible. Return the sliced meat to the reduced broth and hold warm until ready to serve.

Plate the tongue slices, and garnish with the micro-greens drizzled with balsamic.

NOTE: For plating, we only use organic balsamic vinegar from Monticello, New Mexico (p. 211). As remarkable as it may seem, their balsamic compares to the finest Modena balsamic and is crafted in the traditional manner, with no boiling or added sugar.

PAPAS RELLENOS

Besides cooking, the other passion in my life is climbing—mostly big-mountain alpine climbing, but also rocks, ice, buildings, bridges . . . Years ago I did a climbing trip to Peru to climb Alpamayo and I spent a few weeks out in the camps, scaling one of the most perfect mountains in the world. I returned from my climb to the nearest mountain town, Huaraz, where I had less than $3 US to my name. Poor planning meant that I had to feed myself and return to Lima on less than what it would take to get a burger in the States. I found chifas—cheap Chinese stir-fry joints—but even they were too expensive for me since I was emaciated from being on the mountain and needed massive caloric intake. Then, as the sun began to set, kitchen windows throughout town opened, shutters were flung outward, and little handmade signs proclaiming papas rellenos were hung. For the equivalent of 30 cents, I was able to get a meat-filled fried potato that was as big as any steakhouse baked potato. Literally, stuffed Peruvian potatoes saved my life. Ever since, I have made these for travelers and when I'm cooking receptions for clients on a budget.

SPICY BERRY SAUCE

150 g (1 cup) currants, raspberries, or other foraged berries
120 ml (½ cup) chardonnay, room temperature
2 tbsp sugar
1 tsp salt
1 tsp cayenne pepper
1 tbsp butter
salt and pepper, to taste

RELLENOS

185 g (1 cup) foraged Russian olives (p. 205)
2-inch stick cinnamon
1 whole nutmeg
90 g (½ cup) dried apricots
80 g (½ cup) carrot, finely chopped
80 g (½ cup) onion, finely chopped
80 g (½ cup) red bell pepper, finely chopped
454 g (1 lb) ground bison or elk
908 g (2 lb) Yukon gold potatoes, peeled
2 eggs
1 garlic clove, minced
salt and pepper, to taste

MAKE SPICY BERRY SAUCE:

Combine the berries and chardonnay in a saucepan and bring to a simmer. Cook for 15 minutes. Run the mixture through a sieve to remove all solid matter. Return the liquid to the saucepan and add the sugar, salt, and cayenne. Bring to a simmer and reduce by half. Add the butter and whisk until incorporated. Adjust the seasoning and hold until ready to serve.

MAKE RELLENOS:

Place the olives in a saucepan with enough water to cover them. In a small skillet, toast the cinnamon and nutmeg until fragrant. Transfer the spices to the olive pan and bring to a simmer. Cover and simmer for 1 hour. The olives will soften and discolor. Remove from heat, discard the spices, and let the olives cool to room temperature. Place olives in a food processor and grind to a coarse texture. The pits are small enough that they will simply become part of the texture of the dish.

Mince the apricots and stir them into the olives.

In a skillet, sauté the carrot, onion, and bell pepper until softened. Add the meat and brown. Drain off any moisture. Combine the olive mixture with the meat mixture and let cool to room temperature. Adjust seasoning to taste.

Chop the potatoes into large chunks and boil as though making regular mashed potatoes. When soft, drain the water and mash. You want a dry, thick consistency. Add the eggs and garlic and season to taste. Add the butter and mash more aggressively. Allow the potatoes to cool enough to handle.

Liberally dust your hands with the potato starch and grab a golf ball–sized lump of potatoes. Press the ball into a circle that is ¼-inch thick. Add a spoonful of filling to the center of the disk and pull the sides of the disk

56 g (¼ cup) unsalted butter
potato starch, as needed
frying oil

upward to completely encase the filling. Pat the ball to make sure there are no fissures or holes; otherwise, the filling will escape during cooking. Dusting your hands with potato starch will keep the mess from sticking to your hands, but more importantly, it will give a crisp shell to the finished product.

Transfer the formed balls to a plate and store in the refrigerator, letting them firm up for 1 hour.

Heat a pot of frying oil to 350°F. Carefully place the rellenos into the oil two at a time and cook until nicely browned—about 3 minutes. Let rest on a paper towel–lined plate while you make the remaining rellenos. Serve with the spicy berry sauce.

SUGGESTED SUBSTITUTIONS: Pitted green olive is the more traditional ingredient if you don't have access to wild varieties.

JAVELINA BRAISE

The new year means javelina hunting in my neck of the woods, and this tricky meat can turn into a hearty winter meal. You might need to substitute wild boar or locally raised pork, and while a javelina is not the same as domestic pork, the cooking treatment is comparable.

65 ml (¼ cup) olive oil
1816 g (4 lb) javelina roast
640 g (4 cups) onion, chopped
1 whole garlic head, peeled
320 g (2 cups) fresh tomatoes, chopped
2 dried red chiles, whole*
2 bay leaves
salt and pepper, to taste
2 carrots, peeled and chopped
2 sprigs fresh thyme
bottle of hearty red Spanish wine

Preheat the oven to 325°F.

In a large Dutch oven, heat the olive oil. Cut meat into small fist-sized portions. Trimming the fat is a matter of taste—some of these gamey meats, especially javelina, will be funkier than you might like. That funkiness is mostly related to how the meat was handled right after the animal was killed, but the flavor can be mitigated by an overnight milk bath and trimming some fat. If you trim most of the fat, consider adding a pound of pork fat to help maintain moisture.

Sear the meat pieces on all sides in the Dutch oven until browned and crisped. On top of the meat, add the remainder of the ingredients. Cover and braise for 90 minutes. Reduce heat to 225°F and continue cooking for an additional 2 hours. Best served with roasted potatoes and a second bottle of wine.

NOTE: We prefer roasted Hatch red chiles, but use what you have.

SUGGESTED SUBSTITUTIONS: Javelina can be replaced by boar, pig, or any game meat.

JAVELINA PLUM BAKE

I am often inspired by Chef Jesse Griffith of Dai Due in Austin and his commitment to using wild boar. He, like numerous Great Lakes chefs who use invasive species of fish, is making good of a bad thing. Javelinas, like boars and invasive fish, substantially damage the environment, so as you're licking this scrumptious sauce from your fingers, you'll know that you're doing a good thing for Mother Earth.

neutral cooking oil, such as
    canola
1816 g (4 lb) javelina shank or
    roast
160 g (1 cup) onion, chopped
4 garlic cloves, peeled
6 plums, wild if you can find
    them, quartered and pitted
1 bottle chardonnay
salt and pepper, to taste
1 rosemary sprig
135 g (1 cup) walnuts, shelled
2 sweet potatoes, quartered
1 grapefruit, peeled, seeded,
    chopped

Preheat the oven to 325ºF.

Heat enough oil to cover the bottom of a Dutch oven over medium-high heat on your stove. Add the javelina and brown on all sides. Add the onion, garlic, and plums. Pour a glass of chardonnay for yourself and the rest into the pot. Everyone wants to serve deep red wines with game meats, but I prefer a light, acidic wine to cut into the richness of game . . . give it a try, even in the depth of winter! Season with the salt and pepper and bake, covered, in the oven for 1 hour.

Lower the oven to 225ºF and add the rosemary, walnuts, and potatoes. Add water if the liquid has boiled off to maintain an inch of liquid on the bottom. Cover again and return to the oven to bake for 90 more minutes.

Remove from the oven and serve hot with a squeeze of the grapefruit as garnish.

SUGGESTED SUBSTITUTIONS: Javelina can be replaced by boar, pig, or any game meat.

DESERT PRAIRIE RABBIT

The problem with rabbit is that so often it turns out dry. Nothing is worse to me than dry meat slathered in a sauce, attempting to fool you into thinking the meat is juicy. Our foolproof method of making moist, succulent rabbit is an age-old technique—confit. If you use hunted rabbit, be sure to check with the local county extension office for any risks of disease. Otherwise, buy your meat from a reputable source.

hind leg quarters of 2 rabbits, skinned

4 apricots, split in half with pits removed

40 g (¼ cup) coarse salt (we use French gray salt)

szechuan peppercorns

2 sprigs of fresh basil leaves, torn, divided

neutral cooking oil, such as canola

625 g (2 cups) apricot purée

65 ml (¼ cup) shaoxing rice wine

heavy pinch of salt

heavy pinch of sugar

In a large Tupperware container, lay the rabbit legs and split apricots along the bottom. Sprinkle with salt, freshly ground peppercorns, and 1 sprig of the basil. Toss the contents to coat and lay flat in container. Cover tightly and store in the fridge overnight.

On the next day, preheat the oven to 225°F.

Brush the seasoning off the rabbit and apricots, but not too aggressively, leaving bits of the seasoning. Place the items in a roasting pan in a single layer, uncovered. Pour enough oil just to cover the meat. To ensure that you don't spill, place a baking sheet under the roasting pan. Move the pans into the oven and leave for a minimum of 4 and up to 8 hours.

When the rabbit is near ready, combine the purée, shaoxing rice wine, remaining basil, salt, and sugar in a blender and liquefy. Pour the mixture into a small sauce pan and heat until boiling; adjust the seasoning to taste. Serve the rabbit and fruit with the apricot sauce over rice.

SUGGESTED SUBSTITUTIONS: If you don't have access to rabbit, you can use duck or chicken.

DUCK CURRY

There are lots of ingredients in this recipe, but don't be scared off. If you don't have all of the ingredients, either substitute for them or leave them out and make it your own. This curry is the base for a number of our favorite dishes.

RED CURRY BASE

100 g (1 cup) dried red chiles, crushed*
75 g (1 cup) galangal root, roughly chopped with peel
44 g (1 cup) lemongrass (woody exterior removed), chopped
zest of 3 limes
320 g (2 cups) onion, chopped
40 g (½ cup) garlic, whole, peeled
2 tbsp shrimp paste
1 tbsp peppercorns
1 tbsp coriander seeds
1 tsp nutmeg, freshly grated
1 tsp cloves
heavy pinch of salt

DUCK CURRY

4 duck breasts, with skin
1 tbsp neutral cooking oil, such as canola
60 g (¼ cup) red curry base
480 ml (2 cups) coconut milk
2 tbsp brown sugar
2 tbsp fish sauce
80 g (¼ cup) tamarind paste
salt, to taste

MAKE RED CURRY BASE:

Place dried chiles in saucepan with water to cover. Bring to a simmer and cover. Remove from heat and let the chiles soften for 30 minutes. Strain the water into another container. Combine the chiles and all remaining ingredients in a food processor. Process, adding chile water as needed to make it flow like a thick paste. Add the salt.

This curry base can now be stored in your refrigerator for up to a month.

*NOTE: We like to use dried hatch chiles. A more traditional treatment would be dried Thai chiles. But use chiles with the flavor and heat that you enjoy.

MAKE DUCK CURRY:

Preheat the oven to 325°F.

Using a sharp knife, cut a hashtag pattern into the skin of the duck breast. Heat a cast-iron skillet over medium-high heat and add the oil. While the skillet is still cool, add the duck breast, skin-side down. Let cook until the skin is chestnut brown and crisp.

While the duck is rendering, place curry base, coconut milk, sugar, fish sauce, and tamarind paste in a blender and blend until smooth. Add salt to taste, knowing that the sauce will cook down, and err on the side of less salt.

When duck is crisped, remove the duck and place it skin-side up in a small baking dish, pouring curry sauce all around and stopping before you hit the skin. This will allow you to get the curry flavor in the meat but keep the skin crisp. Place the baking dish in the preheated oven, uncovered, and bake for 60 minutes. Lower temperature to 225°F and bake for an additional 90 minutes. Serve hot over rice.

CURRY RICE BALLS

Customers regularly say, "These are amazing, but you only give us one." After hearing that for the millionth time, a regular said it, so I made a wager. I asked him how many he could eat if I made them. He responded, "Easily a dozen." I told him that if he ate a dozen, his whole meal was on me, but if he couldn't, then he had to buy me a night on the town. After seven balls (that I cheated by making extra spicy and larger than normal), he petered—and I enjoyed a nice, expensive night in Phoenix.

CURRY RICE BALLS

275 g (2 cups) cashew pieces
185 g (1 cup) crawfish tails, cleaned
1 (2-inch) piece fresh lemongrass (woody exterior removed), chopped
1-inch piece fresh ginger, roughly chopped
2 tbsp Red Curry Base (p. 74)
130 ml (½ cup) boiling water
salt, to taste
75 g (½ cup) cooked rice
75 g (½ cup) shredded coconut
40 g (½ cup) panko bread crumbs
65 g (½ cup) flour
2 eggs, whisked
65 ml (¼ cup) fish sauce
65 ml (¼ cup) rice wine vinegar
2 tbsp palm sugar (or brown sugar)
1 tbsp cayenne pepper
neutral cooking oil, for frying
fresh mango, chopped

MAKE CURRY RICE BALLS:

In a food processor, combine the cashews through the Red Curry Base. Process just enough to keep a rough texture. Add the boiling water and process until moist but not runny. Taste and season with salt. Cover and chill for 30 minutes or overnight.

Combine rice, coconut, and panko in a bowl. In two separate bowls, add flour to one and whisked eggs to the other. You will have three bowls total (rice mixture, eggs, and flour). Roll the cashew paste into golf ball–sized portions and coat in flour, then egg, and finally the rice mixture. Gently reshape without compacting the outer coating. Chill for 30 minutes or more.

Combine the fish sauce, rice wine vinegar, sugar, and cayenne.

Heat 3 inches of oil in a large saucepan to 350°F.

Deep fry rice balls until golden brown. Serve with fresh mango. Finish with a squirt of the fish sauce mixture. These are great by themselves or on a bed of salad greens.

SUGGESTED SUBSTITUTIONS: You can replace the crawfish with small shrimp.

GOAT MOLE

Goat was my gateway meat to using locally raised animals. If you get well-raised goats that are relatively young (less than a year), then the meat will be tender and not too pungent. And if you're willing to go the extra mile of processing your own meat, they are easy enough to handle since they typically come in at less than a hundred pounds. Mole is a great way of using goat because it will complement the flavor for those who enjoy goat and mask the flavor for those who don't.

MOLE COLORADO

10–15 New Mexico red chiles, dried
4–6 ancho chiles, dried
olive oil
1 tbsp cloves
2 tbsp black pepper, freshly ground
1 tbsp dried oregano
1-inch cinnamon stick, freshly ground
320 g (2 cups) onion, chopped
4 garlic cloves, peeled
50 g (¼ cup) lard
30 g (¼ cup) raisins
135 g (1 cup) almonds, whole
65 g (½ cup) sesame seeds
1440 g (6 cups) crushed tomatoes
1 Mexican chocolate disc
2 tbsp cayenne pepper
64 g (½ cup) cocoa powder
2 tbsp salt, or to taste
1800 g (4 lb) goat meat, trimmed of excess fat and sliced into chunks

MAKE MOLE COLORADO:

Remove the stems and seeds of the chiles and roast them in a dry skillet until smoky. Boil a small stockpot of water and add the toasted dried chiles. Submerge the chiles, cover, and let soak for 30 minutes off the heat.

Heat enough olive oil to coat the bottom of a large stockpot. Add the cloves through garlic and sauté until the onions have softened slightly. Now add the lard through the salt to the stockpot and stir well. Cook for 30 minutes on a simmer. Put the mixture in a blender with 1 cup of the chile water and all of the soaked chiles. Blend until smooth, adding chile water as necessary to create a tomato soup–like consistency. Return the mixture to the stockpot and simmer. Continue simmering for no less than 1 hour and ideally 3 or more hours, stirring regularly to avoid burning. Adjust the salt to taste.

To prepare the goat mole, sear chunked goat meat in hot oil in a large Dutch oven, turning to brown on all sides. Pour enough mole to cover the meat and toss to coat. Bring to a simmer, reduce heat, cover, and let cook for 2 hours. Best served with fried plantain and rice.

SUGGESTED SUBSTITUTIONS: Any meat will work here. In the restaurant, we regularly use chicken, lamb, and pork, but goat is my favorite.

KOREAN ELK

Korean pepper sauce is the base for two of our most popular recipes: braised elk shank and Korean cauliflower. The taste of elk can vary greatly by the habitat of the animal, and often people find it too gamey to enjoy. However, this sweet and spicy sauce tames the flavor and pulls out the delightful aspects of elk, making it a sure hit for your dinner. The elk and cauliflower can be enjoyed together or separately.

KOREAN PEPPER SAUCE
180 g (½ cup) Korean pepper paste (gochujang)
125 ml (½ cup) sesame oil
110 g (½ cup) sugar
125 ml (½ cup) water
65 g (½ cup) sesame seeds, toasted
2 tbsp yellow miso
3 tbsp rice wine vinegar
4 garlic cloves, peeled

KOREAN BRAISED ELK SHANK
neutral oil
salt and pepper, to taste
6 elk shank, cut into 2-inch-thick portions
575 g (2 cups) Korean Pepper Sauce

KOREAN CAULIFLOWER
neutral oil
2 cauliflower heads
575 g (2 cups) Korean sauce

MAKE KOREAN PEPPER SAUCE:

Combine all of the sauce ingredients in the blender and process until smooth. The sesame seeds will remain whole in the final sauce. Adjust for sweetness, heat, and saltiness.

MAKE KOREAN BRAISED ELK SHANK:

Heat a roasting pan to medium-high on the stovetop while preheating the oven to 325°F. Add a light coating of neutral oil to the bottom of the pan and bring to just smoking. Season the elk with salt and pepper. Add the meats, cut-side down, and sear until a nice dark-brown crust forms. Turn the meat and crust the other side. Pour the Korean Pepper Sauce over the browned meat, cover with foil, and bake in the oven for 1 hour. After 1 hour has passed, lower the temperature to 225°F and continue baking for at least 3 hours or until the meat is fall-off-the-bone tender. Add sauce as necessary and salt to taste. Best served with roasted potatoes.

MAKE KOREAN CAULIFLOWER:

Preheat the oven to 450°F.

Coat a baking sheet with neutral cooking oil. Cut the cauliflower into ½-inch slices, trying your best to keep the slices intact, although they will inevitably crumble. Lay the slices in a single layer across the pan. Coat with more oil—be generous, not healthy! Bake for 20 minutes. Turn the cauliflower over (this is why we try to keep it in big pieces) and bake an additional 20 minutes. Turn one more time and continue cooking until the cauliflower becomes dark brown. Near the end, brush the Korean Pepper Sauce generously over the cauliflower and return to the oven for 5 more minutes. Lightly salt and serve.

SUGGESTED SUBSTITUTIONS: You can replace the elk with venison, boar, javelina, or in a pinch, beef.

MEXICAN DRINKING CHOCOLATE

Early in my career, I was challenged by an online blogger, Martin Lersch, and his TGRWT (They Go Really Well Together) competitions. This monthly event used flavor pairing science to present ingredients that would seem to contradict, but left it to the participants to find ways to make it work. I call those days my "Shock and Awe" Days! Most of those recipes have been relegated to history, but a few have stood the test of time and have inspired numerous modern dishes.

SALMON MARSHMALLOWS

1 packet or can of dry-smoked salmon
125 ml (½ cup) neutral cooking oil, such as canola
8 sheets silver gelatin (2 tbsp & 2 tsp powdered), softened
65 ml (¼ cup) corn syrup, lightly warmed in microwave
150 g (¾ cup) sugar
3 tbsp corn syrup, room temperature

DRINKING CHOCOLATE

75 g (½ cup) 75% chocolate chips
500 ml (2 cups) water
1 cinnamon stick, toasted
1 clove, freshly ground
1 juniper berry
70 g (½ cup) hackberries, dried (p. 34)
2-inch orange peel strip

MAKE SALMON MARSHMALLOWS:

Place the salmon, its juices, and oil in a small saucepan and heat to just warm. With the stove on its absolute lowest setting, cover and let steep 30 minutes. Strain the oil through a coffee filter and enjoy the salmon on a salad. Set the salmon-flavored oil aside.

Place the gelatin and the warmed corn syrup in the bowl of a mixer fitted with a whisk attachment. In a saucepan over medium heat, add the sugar and room-temperature corn syrup, and cook to 230°F. Pour the hot syrup over the warmed syrup and gelatin in the mixing bowl and mix on medium-high speed. When the marshmallow begins to increase in volume, drizzle the salmon oil, continuing to whisk until the marshmallow is cool to the touch—about 10 minutes. Quickly spread the marshmallow onto a Silpat-lined baking sheet. Let the marshmallow set up—around 30 minutes—and cut into cubes for serving.

MAKE DRINKING CHOCOLATE:

Combine all of the ingredients in a saucepan and heat until simmering. Cover and steep the liquid for 15 minutes; then, strain out all of the solids. Return to heat and simmer until reduced slightly and thickened to a cream-like consistency. Adjust to taste with sugar and serve with the salmon marshmallow.

HACKBERRY BACON BONBONS

This is my twist on the tried-and-true restaurant appetizer of bacon and dates. Truly one of my favorite chocolates to make!

   30

125 ml (½ cup) cream, plus more as needed

135 g (1 cup) hackberries, dried (p. 34)

3 tbsp sugar

vanilla pod, split with seeds scraped

75 g (½ cup) 75% chocolate chips

150 g (1 cup) milk chocolate, chopped

1 tbsp bourbon

56 g (¼ cup) unsalted butter, softened

38 g (¼ cup) bacon, cooked to crisp and finely minced

In a small saucepan, heat cream and hackberries until simmering. Remove from heat, cover, and let steep for 1 hour. Strain the berries out and add additional cream to return the amount to 112 grams. Bring to a simmer and hold.

In medium saucepan, melt the sugar until a light caramel forms. Add the vanilla pod and seeds to the caramel and continue cooking until a medium caramel is made. Carefully pour the hot cream through a strainer into the caramel, removing the vanilla pod, and whisk until smooth. Remove from heat and let rest 1 minute.

In a food processor, grind the two chocolates into small pebbles. Pour the caramel sauce over the chocolates and process until smooth. Add the bourbon and butter and process until homogenous. Add the bacon and briefly incorporate. Transfer to a pastry bag and cool to room temperature. Pipe into prepared chocolate molds and let set up overnight. Spread a thin layer of tempered chocolate onto the bottom of the molds to cap the bonbons; allow to set firm and serve.

SUGGESTED SUBSTITUTIONS: Replace dates for hackberries equally by weight.

HOW TO PREPARE A CHOCOLATE MOLD

Chocolate molds are available online or at most hobby stores. The rigid polycarbonate molds are easier to use and produce a better final product, but even the flexible silicon molds will do the job. Be sure that the mold is clean and completely dry.

Using a ladle scoop tempered chocolate and pour it onto the mold, filling the cavities with the chocolate. Rotate the mold around, keeping the cavities facing upward, and spread the chocolate with the bottom of the ladle to make sure that each cavity is filled. Gently rap the mold on a counter to remove air bubbles. Wait approximately one minute for the chocolate to adhere to the mold. A colder room will set faster, and a warmer room will take longer.

Once the chocolate is sticking to the mold, but before the center of each cavity is firming, turn the mold upside down pouring the chocolate back into the bowl of unused tempered chocolate. Using an offset spatula or a butter knife, scrape the mold so that a thin layer of chocolate remains in each cavity but the excess has been removed. The mark of a good chocolatier is the ability to get a shell that is as thin as possible while still being structurally strong enough to be filled and handled. Place the mold on a cookie sheet and then transfer it to the refrigerator for 10 minutes to set solid. The mold is now prepared and ready for the fillings in this book.

HOW TO TEMPER CHOCOLATE

Tempering chocolate is, at its most basic level, a combination of heating chocolate to remove bad crystals, cooling chocolate to add good crystals, and then warming the chocolate to make it pourable. Only practice can make your chocolates perfectly shiny and crisp time after time. Here are the basic steps for the beginning chocolatier.

Weigh out 454 g (1 pound) of dark chocolate. Heat the chocolate in a double boiler over a very low heat, stirring slowly but regularly, until the chocolate is melted and at 115°F. Be sure to not allow water from the double boiler to touch the chocolate or any of the surfaces or tools in the process or the chocolate will seize and be ruined. Pour the melted chocolate on a marble or granite slab and, using a putty knife or offset spatula, spread and scrape the chocolate in all directions, bringing the temperature down to 82°F. Return the chocolate to the double boiler and stir consistently until the temperature rises to 90°F. The chocolate is now ready to be poured into your mold.

ELK'S BLOOD BONBONS

Not for the faint of heart, and one of those things that it's better not to tell your guests what they're eating, but the high minerality of the elk and the black cocoa make for one heck of a flavor. Don't just save this for Halloween; give it to your sweetie for Valentine's Day too!

Fresh elk heart
85 g (1 cup) black cocoa powder
125 ml (½ cup) cream
110 g (½ cup) sugar
2 tbsp corn syrup
150 g (1 cup) milk chocolate chips (see chocolate tempering on p. 85)

Pat the elk heart as dry as is possible. Douse the heart with the cocoa powder, stuffing the powder in every nook, cranny, and ventricle. Vacuum seal the heart, and cook the heart sous vide for 24 hours at 176°F.

Remove the heart from the bag and chop it into large chunks. Place the chunks in your food processor and grind into a rough mass, like ground meat. Do not turn the heart into a purée. Place the ground meat in a strainer and let the juice drip into a cup, coaxing with a spoon if necessary, but trying to gather only liquid, not solids. You want to end up with 125 g (½ cup) of cocoa-elk liquid.

Combine cocoa-elk liquid and cream in a medium saucepan. Bring to a simmer and let simmer 2 minutes. Hold warm. In a stainless steel or copper pan, melt the sugar and corn syrup over medium-high heat. Stir very gently as the sugar begins to caramelize. Cook to a light golden brown. Carefully strain the hot blood cream into the caramel. Whisk gently until a creamy, loose caramel sauce is obtained. Let rest 5 minutes.

Grind the chocolate in a food processor until small pebbles are formed. (You should have already cleaned out the chopped up heart from the processor bowl!) Pour the blood cream over the chocolate and let rest for 2 minutes, then process until smooth. Transfer to a piping bag and fill prepared chocolate molds, allowing them to set up overnight. Spread a thin layer of tempered chocolate onto the bottom of the molds to cap the bonbons; allow to set firm and serve.

SUGGESTED SUBSTITUTIONS: Beef heart can be used in place of elk.

SUGAR CREAM PIE

For Indiana Hoosiers, this is about as comfort-food as it gets. Not fancy, not healthy, but what's an old dairy farmer to do with all that leftover cream?

500 ml (2 cups) cream
125 ml (½ cup) half-and-half
110 g (½ cup) sugar
40 g (¼ cup + 1 tbsp) all-
    purpose flour
pinch of salt
1 baked pie shell
1 tsp nutmeg, freshly grated
Bacon Jam (p. 53)

Preheat the oven to 425°F.

Combine the cream, half-and-half, sugar, flour, and salt in a large, glass measuring cup. Microwave in 1-minute blasts on high until the liquid becomes hot, but not boiling. Pour into the pie shell, sprinkle with nutmeg, and bake for 10 minutes. Reduce the oven to 350°F and bake until lightly set—about 50 minutes. Cool to room temperature and serve with a dollop of Bacon Jam.

3 | FROM THE FARM (DOMESTIC PLANTS)

PROFILE: NAAVA KOENIGSBERG:
Ethical Wildcrafting

by Andrea Feucht

Naava Koenigsberg, an herbalist in Silver City, sits before me in the coffee shop, cross-legged and smiling—a radiant woman. In the middle of the interview, she is talking about how we, as modern Westerners from America's desert Southwest, can interact more directly with our food and our natural world.

These days, it's easy to fall into pessimism about our future prospects for sustainable eating and health. Naava avoids that pit of negativity. She sees a way to guide many of us back to the connection we crave with our health and our food.

We start at the beginning of our personal food knowledge, as toddlers. Most of us learned our ideas about food from our parents. This is an idea that Michael Pollan wrote about a decade or more ago. He says we were told as kids by parents, "Eat your vegetables because I said so!" We grumbled, and some of us complied. But over time, new food mantras made their way into our ears from outside experts like celebrity doctors, the media, and food packaging. The new messages said, "Eat your carrots because they have beta carotene!" With that, a fundamental shift occurred—we are taking food advice from authority figures, but we have no personal relationship with those authorities, nor do they with us. Those experts have no accountability for our health, no way to know on a person-by-person basis whether they are doing good.

Here is where proponents of wildcrafting, the art of harvesting wild foods and medicines, come into the picture. As benevolent purveyors of food wisdom, they serve as intermediaries between the wild and the domesticated. As we talk, Naava describes a kind of expertise beyond parents and consumer culture, a potential source of wise guidance on what to eat and when to eat it: local restaurants. By serving wholesome dishes with wild and locally sourced ingredients, chefs increasingly are taking on the advice-giving role through their cooking, coaching, "Eat this because it is delicious, local, and good for you."

This is where Rob enters Naava's story as a chef and as a responsible forager. At the beginning of his relationship with Naava, Rob sought general knowledge of what wild plants to use in his cooking and how to gather them safely, ethically, and responsibly. As they grew to know each other, they exchanged knowledge—Naava's plant expertise and Rob's creativity with local ingredients—to play on the idea that restaurants can be forces for good in human lives, not just places to spend money and consume calories.

Naava spent many years learning the complexities of wild and cultivated herbs on both coasts, as well as in Guatemala, then did more travel before landing in Silver City. From her mentors and teachers, she learned *ethical wildcrafting*.

Ethical wildcrafting means harvesting wild plants in a manner that honors the earth, the plants, the food, and the community. Sustainable wildcrafting means harvesting in a manner that ensures that the plant stands will be healthy and vibrant long into the future. Responsible wildcrafting is both ethical and sustainable because you are being acutely aware of your own intentions and paying attention to what the plants and land communicate back to you.

Naava's first teacher, Pam Montgomery, taught her that having a real relationship with wild food means searching beyond the merely edible. Just because a plant won't kill you if you eat it doesn't mean that it will be enjoyable. Many wild foods have been eaten in times of hardship because they provide sustenance. But there is a plethora of wild food out there that, especially when properly prepared, is absolutely delicious!

Rob's hope when Naava tastes a new dish is that her opinion will land solidly in the yummy category—even if the combination of ingredients seems strange.

Naava, Rob, and others in their spheres, interweave their thoughts, practices, and actions to create a holistic sustainable food community. They share a common inspiration: that seeking and making connections between humans and the natural world are of prime importance. Humans have spent nearly all of history in a close working relationship with the natural world, only to have that change during the last several hundred years. We seem to thrive at many levels when we reestablish that contact, even in this modern world.

Our modern conveniences do not have to be a one-way ticket to marginal health and divorce from the natural world. Naava believes that now is the perfect time for chefs like Rob to be native-food proponents and facilitators. Dry attempts at nutrition education will persuade few, but chefs' engagement with their ingredients and with their customers gives them the authority they can use to change hearts and minds . . . and stomachs.

PROFILE: KYLE SKAGGS AND MEGGIE DEXTER:

Work Their Land

by Andrea Feucht

Meggie Dexter curls up in the chair opposite me in my favorite Silver City coffee shop, the one that doesn't offer WiFi but rather has stacks of magazines and copies of the *New York Times*, and begins the conversation by handing me snap beans from the farm. It's the middle of the summer and, by all accounts, Frisco Farm, where she lives and works with Kyle Skaggs, is beginning to enter peak season.

Meggie grew up in a New Hampshire family governed by the twin pillars of frugality and food quality, where the garden was the produce department and the chicken coop was the meat counter. One night, she and her siblings came home to a note from their mom about where to find dinner: "There's chicken in the fridge and salad in the garden." As a kid, the nose-to-tail practices occasionally crossed a threshold: for a long time, Meggie was averse to stewed chicken feet,

but even on that, she's come around—the resulting broth is just too good. She laughs when she tells me about the first time she and Kyle made it: "I made him peel the feet!"

As a young adult with her own landscaping business, Meggie nudged clients toward adding vegetables to their flower beds or as replacement for their vast tracts of sod. Even with her natural charm and botanical knowledge, it was an uphill battle; after a few years she was ready to move on to something more sustainable, less decorative. She traveled a bit, landing in Silver City with family over the holidays in 2008. The sun and the climate were alluring, and she decided to stay to work with Americorps doing trail maintenance for several months. After that stint, she picked up a job at the food co-op, but she wasn't satisfied working indoors. And then, it happened. Kyle Skaggs walked in the door of the co-op with his

Frisco bounty, and Meggie was ready to make the leap to go back to working the land. Over the course of a year, she grew a relationship of mutual respect with Kyle and his work, ultimately taking the role as Frisco Farm's right-hand woman. She kept her part-time co-op job—she really believes in what they do, the mission they serve—but most of the time she's at the farm, a short one-hour drive from Silver City.

Frisco Farm started out with a sunny future built in—they're in a river valley with excellent water rights, something we in the West value almost more than our sunshine. With ample water and good soil, they've been able to choose not to use tractors in the farm work, relying instead on two draft horses to work the land when needed. Horses are not cheaper than tractors, but it feels good to buy feed as fuel rather than petroleum.

The relationship between Rob and Frisco Farm began not with the local farmers' market but with buying meats and groceries from The Curious Kumquat when it was a gourmet shop. Later on, at the full-blown restaurant, on a rare night out for dinner, Kyle and Meggie realized someone gave a shit about the quality of ingredients served, from meat to vegetables and everything in between. The business relationship began with lettuce. Lots and lots of lettuce. These days, Rob still procures his greens from Frisco, but supplements with anything particularly shiny or fab-ulous at the farmers' market, with butternut squash and purple potatoes being recent favorites.

Their favorite crop—the underdog they'd like to sing from the rooftops—is celeriac. Meggie loves to use it in stews as an alternative to celery or even potatoes. Garlic is another favorite: easy to grow and easy to sell, they could practically support the whole farm on just garlic profits. Meggie and Kyle see Frisco evolving over the next few years by digging deep, literally—producing more root and hardy veggies, like beets and turnips and carrots and cabbage.

Farming, to Meggie, is a cause. It makes the world more productive in the sense that they are creating value rather than consuming. They love being self-sufficient, even if it is tiring. Kyle is a little more pragmatic—he appreciates what they do and he loves the work, but he jokes about how it's all well and good "until you get run over by your horses!"

But the best moment, the one that makes Kyle and Meggie grin in delight and even choke up a bit, is the farmers' market. They've worked so hard to grow great food. They pack it all up and bring it to town, and when they arrive to set up, there's already a line of their devoted customers eager to see what's ripe this week, waiting with their canvas sacks, waiting just for them. Meggie's voice cracks as she smiles, overcome with emotion. That's why the two of them feel they've found their place, at least for now.

HUITLACOCHE BUTTERNUT SOUP

How can any self-respecting chef resist serving smut! Each fall, local farmers bring me their blight, their rot, their fungus. The star of the rot fest is huitlacoche (cuitlaçoche), also known as corn smut. Corn farmers don't like seeing it . . . till I give them a wad of cash for their smut (almost always handed over in an unmarked brown paper bag). Also known as Mexican truffle, this odd ingredient can be found canned or frozen, but if you're lucky, you'll get it fresh. Use as you would mushrooms or truffle.

MISO SOIL
90 g (1 cup) almond meal or flour
56 g (¼ cup) butter, room
     temperature
70 g (¼ cup) yellow miso
2 tbsp dehydrated miso powder
½ tsp salt

RABBIT STOCK
neutral oil
1 onion, peeled
1 carrot, peeled
2 celery stalks
1 head of garlic
1 rabbit carcass (leftover from
     other recipes where most of
     the meat has been removed)
2 tbsp salt
2 tbsp black peppercorns, whole
2 tbsp fennel seed
1 stick cinnamon

MAKE MISO SOIL:

Preheat the oven to 225°F.

Combine almond meal, butter, and yellow miso in a mixing bowl and cream the mixture with a rubber spatula. Spread the mixture on a Silpat-lined baking sheet to a ⅛-inch thickness. Bake for 20 to 30 minutes, being sure to not allow the dough to brown. Remove from the oven and immediately add the miso powder and salt. Crumble the dough between the palms of your hands and let cool to room temperature. Store in an airtight container for up to 2 weeks.

MAKE RABBIT STOCK:

To a large stockpot, add enough oil to coat the bottom of the pan. Coarsely chop onion, carrot, and celery stalks. Take the garlic head and take off any of the papery skin that removes easily, leaving the rest. Cut through the garlic horizontally and toss it in the pot. Chop the rabbit carcass into a few large sections; add it to the pot. Cook on medium-high, stirring from time to time, until the rabbit browns slightly and the vegetables begin to soften just a bit. Color means flavor, so don't be shy about how much you cook the ingredients, but be sure to stop before burning anything. Just before you're done browning, add the salt and peppercorns, the fennel seed, and cinnamon stick. Stir the pot to get the spices mixed in with the rabbit and vegetables and toast until the cinnamon becomes fragrant. Fill your pot one inch short of the top with water and return to the heat. Bring to a boil and immediately reduce to a simmer. Cook for 2 hours at a simmer, skimming and discarding any foam that forms on the top.

After 2 hours, adjust the salt, stir, and then pour the stock through a strainer into a second stockpot. Pick the remaining meat from the carcass to use in a soup, and discard all of the other ingredients. Let the stock sit until it gets to room temperature. The stock can be used or stored in the refrigerator for later use.

HUITLACOCHE BUTTERNUT SOUP

2 tbsp olive oil

80 g (½ cup) onion, chopped

1 garlic clove, peeled

650 g (4 cups) butternut
squash, peeled, seeded,
chopped

2 liters (9 cups) Rabbit Stock (p. 98)

25 g (¼ cup) huitlacoche,
chopped

1 sprig fresh thyme

salt, to taste

MAKE HUITLACOCHE BUTTERNUT SOUP:

Heat oil in a medium stockpot. Add the onion and sauté until soft but not browned. Add the garlic and continue sautéing for 1 minute. Add the squash and cook for 5 minutes. Pour the Rabbit Stock into the pot and bring to a simmer. Once bubbling, add the huitlacoche and thyme. Gently boil uncovered for 30 minutes or until the butternut is tender.

Remove and discard the thyme sprig and transfer the soup to a blender (depending on the size of the blender, this may take multiple batches). Process until smooth and hold until ready to serve.

To serve, ladle the soup into a shallow bowl and place a freshly baked Acorn Financier (p. 162) in center of bowl. Sprinkle on the Miso Soil, a dollop of Sweet Corn Butter (p. 193) and puffed amaranth (p. 166).

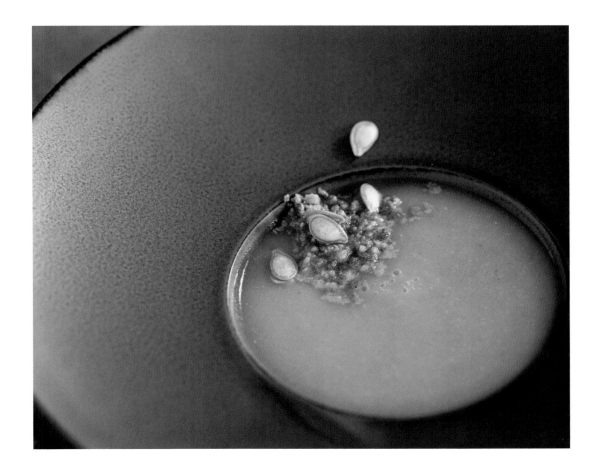

CURRIED KUMQUAT CHUTNEY

I love kumquats, with their sweet and tart juice explosion. They go great with so many things, both sweet and savory. I also like to preserve this chutney in jars and give it to my friends for holiday gifts.

   10

110 g (½ cup) sugar
62 g (¼ cup) rice vinegar
1 tbsp candied ginger, chopped
1 tbsp dried cranberries, chopped
2 tbsp sumac (p. 36)
1 tsp madras curry powder
240 g (1½ cups) kumquats
2 tbsp cilantro, chopped
habanero pepper, to taste
salt, to taste

Combine the sugar, vinegar, ginger, cranberries, sumac, and curry powder in a saucepan. Chop kumquats in half along their equator. While many people enjoy the seeds, I prefer to spend a few minutes removing the seeds. To deseed, pinch the kumquat half and roll between your fingers. The seeds will pop right out. Rough chop the kumquats and place 1 cup of them in the saucepan. Cook over medium heat until reduced to about 1 cup (about 10 minutes). Transfer the contents to a bowl and chill. Chop and add the remaining kumquats, cilantro, habanero, and salt. Chill and serve.

SUGGESTED SUBSTITUTIONS: Lemon rind would replace the sumac well here, kicking up the tartness a bit.

QUINOA GRATIN

I love farmer ingenuity. I love when a farmer is willing to commit valuable acreage to crops that have questionable sellability but potential. When I lived in Alamosa, Colorado, there were farmers trying to raise quinoa because of its success in the Andes of South America and the geographic similarities of the region. At that point, few knew what quinoa was and hardly a farmer knew that the crop could replace traditional crops, such as potatoes. Nearly twenty years later, quinoa has been firmly established and has provided nutrition and livelihoods to many residents of that remote community.

QUINOA CAKES
1 tbsp neutral cooking oil, such as canola
40 g (¼ cup) shallot, minced
128 g (1 cup) quinoa, dry
1 tsp salt
32 g (¼ cup) flour
1 egg

SALT-BAKED LEEKS
908 g (2 lb) kosher salt
2 leeks

GARLIC SOUP
2 tbsp butter
160 g (1 cup) onion, chopped
160 g (1 cup) garlic, peeled
1 liter (4½ cups) Rabbit Stock (p. 98)
120 g (2 cups) day-old bread, torn into chunks
1 bay leaf
salt, to taste
125 ml (½ cup) half-and-half
black pepper, ground, to taste

MAKE QUINOA CAKES:

Heat oil in a medium saucepan and add the shallots. Sauté the shallots until they turn translucent. Add the quinoa and toss to coat. Fill the pan with water, bring to a boil, and cook as if it were pasta. Boil for 10 minutes. Drain the quinoa very well and transfer to a mixing bowl. Add the salt, flour, and egg, and mix everything together.

Line a baking sheet with parchment paper. Using a 3-inch ring mold, press ½ inch of quinoa into a firm, flattened disk. Remove the mold and continue until all of the quinoa mixture is used. Store in the refrigerator to allow the quinoa cakes to set up.

MAKE SALT-BAKED LEEKS:

Preheat the oven to 350°F.

Pour ½ inch of salt on the bottom of a loaf pan. Make two cuts on each leek. The first is to remove the bottom roots—cut ½ inch off the root bottoms. The second is to remove the top—cut where the white transitions to green on the outer layers. The tops can be used in stock or turned into an ash (p. 191). Do not remove the outer layers, as they will protect the tender insides during cooking.

Lay the two trimmed leeks on the salt bed and cover with the remaining salt, making sure that none of the leek shows through. Ideally, the leek will be covered at all spots by ½-inch of salt to insulate it from the heat. Bake for 1 hour. Remove the pan from the oven, but leave the leeks buried to continue baking and infusing flavor until ready to serve.

MAKE GARLIC SOUP:

Melt the butter in a stockpot. Add the onion and garlic and cook over a medium-low heat until the onions start to brown—don't cook them to caramelized. Add the stock, bread, bay leaf, and salt, and bring to a simmer over medium-high heat. Cook for 15 minutes. Remove the bay leaf and salt to taste. Purée the soup with a blender and return to the heat. Add the half-and-half and black pepper and adjust the seasoning one last time.

AMARANTH PORRIDGE

1 tbsp butter
75 g (1 cup) amaranth seed
1 tbsp brown sugar
1 tsp salt
65 ml (1 cup) Rabbit Stock (p. 98)
2 tbsp cream
neutral oil
4 Quinoa Cakes (previous page)
4 slices provolone cheese
80 g (½ cup) peeled and finely
    diced Granny Smith apple
fresh fennel leaves

MAKE AMARANTH PORRIDGE:

Melt butter in a medium saucepan. Add the amaranth seed and stir until a nutty brown aroma hits your nose. Add the sugar, salt, and stock. Bring to a simmer and continue cooking until most of the liquid has been cooked off. Add the cream and hold, covered, until ready to serve.

Preheat your oven's broiler.

Heat a large skillet with a heavy coating of neutral cooking oil over medium-high heat. Carefully add the Quinoa Cakes, making sure not to crowd the skillet. Cook for about 3 minutes and turn to cook the other side. The cakes should have a deep brown crust now.

Spoon a quarter of the Garlic Soup in the center of a large bowl. Place the fried Quinoa Cake in the center. Top with a quarter of the Amaranth Porridge. Remove the leeks from their salt bed and peel off the outer layer until all you see is white flesh. Cut into ½-inch rings and place a few in the porridge. Cover with a slice of provolone and set the bowl under the broiler until the cheese begins to melt. Top with the apples and fennel and dig in.

ROLLED ROASTED ROOTS

Ever since Fred Flintstone had his car turned on its side by the dinosaur ribs at the drive-in, people expect their meat entrée to be monumental. I mean really, a petit filet?! No, you want the 60-ounce prime or the ostrich osso bucco with the leg bone standing high in the air. These dishes make a statement. Meanwhile, your spouse orders a vegetarian meal, which looks like a baby turtle spit up its breakfast.

So I set out to create a vegetarian entrée that could rival the dinosaur ribs and honed in on this simple but big-impact recipe.

CHICKPEA CAKE
500 ml (2 cups) whole milk
2 tbsp olive oil
2 tbsp unsalted butter, melted
2 tsp salt
125 g (1 cup) chickpea flour, sifted
zest of 1 lemon
neutral oil, for frying

ROLLED ROOTS
1 medium-sized beet, peeled
1 medium-sized turnip, peeled
1 medium-sized potato, peeled
1 large carrot, peeled
salt and pepper, to taste
neutral oil

BÉCHAMEL SAUCE
2 tbsp butter
2 tbsp flour
315 ml (1¼ cups) milk, heated
salt and pepper, to taste

*NOTE: A Chiba peeler is a Japanese rotary peeler that will create one long, continuous strip of vegetables.

MAKE CHICKPEA CAKE:

Combine the milk and oil in a large saucepan and bring to a simmer. Add the melted butter and stir. In a mixing bowl, whisk the salt and sifted chickpea flour. Slowly shake the chickpea flour mixture into the simmering milk, whisking constantly to avoid lumps from forming. The highest risk of lumps is at the beginning, so be very aggressive with your whisking and very subtle with your chickpea flour addition. Once all of the *chickpea flour has been added, and thoroughly whisked, reduce the heat to medium to evaporate as much liquid as you can from the thick batter. The batter will start with a cake-batter consistency, but within a few minutes of the higher heat it should thicken to a thick grits or oatmeal texture. Cook for approximately 5 minutes, slowly but consistently scraping the bottom of the pan. Remove the pan from the heat and add the lemon zest.

Line a loaf pan with plastic wrap leaving enough excess to completely cover the loaf pan a second time, but letting the excess hang over onto the counter. Scrape the chickpea batter into the pan and spread the batter to create a smooth surface. Fold the excess plastic wrap back over the pan, pressing it into the batter, ensuring that no air reaches the batter. Refrigerate for at least 1 hour and up to 2 days.

MAKE ROLLED ROOTS:

Preheat the oven to 425°F.

Prepare the vegetables by chopping off the stem ends and cutting each to a length of 3 inches. Run each vegetable through a Chiba* peeler, resulting in 4–8-inch strips of each that are roughly 3 inches wide. If you don't have access to a Chiba peeler, carefully peel the vegetables with a regular hand peeler, doing your best to keep long, continuous strips. Keep the core of the potato to serve as the faux osso bucco bone.

Using a 3-foot section of your counter, lay the beet strip down first. Directly on top of the beet, lay the turnip, the potato, and then the carrot so you'll have all four vegetables stacked on top of each other. Sprinkle the stack with salt and pepper and place the potato core at one end of the strip. Begin rolling the core toward the opposite end, wrapping the strips around the core, which will build rather quickly in thickness. When you get to the

end of the strip, stand the roll on its flattest side and use a toothpick to secure the end of the roll. Repeat the process until all of the strips are used.

Lightly coat the bottom of a baking pan with oil. Place the rolls in the pan, cover with foil, and bake for 60 minutes or until the core is tender, basting with additional oil two times during the baking process.

MAKE BÉCHAMEL SAUCE:

In a small saucepan, melt the butter over a medium heat. Once melted, add the flour and slowly, but constantly, whisk until the flour is mixed in and smooth. Whisk for 1 more minute, then add the hot milk, a little at a time, whisking constantly, until the thick flour paste loosens into a slurry. Continue whisking slowly while the slurry returns to a boil, reduce the heat to medium-low, and continue cooking for 2 more minutes. Remove from the heat and add the salt and black pepper to taste. Keep the sauce covered until ready to serve.

To serve, fill a deep skillet with ½ inch of neutral oil and heat to 325°F. Using a round cutter or the mouth of a drinking glass, cut the chickpea cake into discs. Fry the cakes until golden brown (about 4 minutes) and then turn to cook the other side. Once both sides are cooked, remove the discs and drain on a paper towel. Transfer the disc to the serving plate, and pour some béchamel sauce on the disc. Place the rolled roots on top of the sauce, remove the toothpick, and enjoy.

POACHED YOLKS

CURED YOLK
480 g (2 cups) fine sea salt
55 g (¼ cup) Okinawa black
    sugar, grated
2 tbsp fennel seed
6 fresh, farmers' market egg
    yolks

ACORN CRUST
cooking oil
125 g (1 cup) acorn flour (p. 32)
½ tsp neutral cooking oil, such
    as canola
½ tsp salt
85 ml (⅓ cup) water

ATXA YOLK WITH FAUX
    MUSHROOM BROTH
2 dosing syringes (can be
    purchased at a pharmacy)
250 ml (1 cup) water
75 g (½ cup) cocoa nibs, lightly
    toasted
1 tbsp yellow miso
salt, to taste
4 g (1 tsp) xanthan gum
6 extremely fresh egg yolks,
    separated from whites

MAKE CURED YOLK:

Combine salt, sugar, and fennel seed in a bowl. In a loaf pan, sprinkle just enough of the salt mixture to coat the bottom evenly to about ¼ inch depth. Carefully lay the yolks on the mixture, keeping an inch of space between each yolk. Gently sprinkle the remaining mixture on top, making sure that the yolks are completely covered. Let sit covered in the refrigerator for a week or until the yolks are firm to the touch. Once firm, remove the yolks, gently brush the salt mixture off, and set on a drying rack. If you have a meat-curing box or a wine cellar, age the yolks for an additional week. Store in a dry, airtight container for up to a year.

MAKE ACORN CRUST:

Preheat the oven to 300°F.

Heat a deep skillet with 1 inch of cooking oil to 350°F.

Combine the acorn flour, oil, and salt in a mixing bowl, rubbing it between the palms of your hands until a coarse sand is formed. Place in the bowl of a stand mixer fitted with the paddle attachment. Begin mixing and gradually add the water until a thick paste is achieved. Spread roughly into a 2-inch square on a Silpat or parchment paper and bake for 10 minutes, or until curled and crisp on the edges. Fry the baked crusts until crisp throughout. Remove to a paper towel to absorb the oil. Hold the crusts in a dry, airtight container until ready to serve.

MAKE ATXA YOLK WITH FAUX MUSHROOM BROTH:

In a small saucepan, combine water, cocoa nibs, and miso. Bring to a simmer. Taste and add salt as needed. Add xanthan gum and mix with an immersion blender to the consistency of a runny egg yolk. Hold at 145°F.

When ready to serve, place the acorn crust on the plate. Gently place an egg yolk in an Asian soup spoon that has been dipped in water to prevent the yolk from sticking to the spoon. Poke the yolk with a toothpick in the top center. Using one of the sterilized dosing syringes, extract ¾ of the yolk filling from the egg by entering at the poked hole, being careful to not pierce the bottom of the yolk. Discard the yolk filling or feed it to your dogs. Immediately fill the second dosing syringe with the hot broth and then gently re-insert the syringe into the top center hole of the yolk. This hot liquid will poach the yolk from the inside out. Stop when the filling starts to ooze from the hole. Carefully pour the yolk from the spoon onto the crust, keeping the toothpick hole on the top of the yolk. If the hole rotates from the top, the filling will ooze from the yolk.

Garnish with Asparagus Soil (p. 198), freshly sautéed asparagus tips, grated Cured Yolk, and arugula microgreens.

BEETS & YOGURT

Many of my dishes straddle the line between sweet and savory. Left to my own devices, I would live off of salted sugar cubes! This dish is one of my favorites for moving guests from their meat courses into dessert, and it's also my test to see how good a sommelier is going to be because the flavors are so complex.

  10

SALT-BAKED BEETS

800 g (4 cups) kosher salt

43 g (½ cup) coffee, ground

2 tbsp fennel seed

2 medium-sized beets, whole, with the top and bottom removed, peel remaining

2 tbsp sugar

250 ml (1 cup) rice vinegar

YOGURT SPHERES

3 tbsp cream

½ sheet silver gelatin (½ tsp powder), softened

1 tbsp maple syrup

250 g (1 cup) Greek yogurt

4 g (1½ tsp) sodium alginate

1 liter (4½ cups) water

SWEET CORN DUKKAH

110 g (1 cup) freeze-dried sweet corn (not frozen corn)

65 g (½ cup) sesame seeds

2 tbsp coriander seeds

2 tbsp cumin seeds

2 tsp freshly ground black pepper

1 tsp flake salt

MAKE SALT-BAKED BEETS:

Preheat the oven to 350°F.

Combine the salt, coffee, and fennel seed in a bowl. In an aluminum loaf pan, pour ½ inch of the salt mixture to cover the bottom. Place the beets leaf-side down on the salt. Cover the beets with the remaining salt mixture, ensuring that no beet is showing through the salt. Place in the oven and bake for 75 minutes, or until tender when poked with a toothpick. Let cool enough to handle.

Using a kitchen towel, rub the skin away from the beets, trimming any sticky skin with a paring knife. Cut the beets into ¼-inch thick sticks.

Dissolve the sugar into the vinegar and place the beet sticks in the vinegar until ready to serve.

MAKE YOGURT SPHERES:

Heat the cream in the microwave on high until warm. Melt the gelatin in the warm cream and add the maple syrup. Add the sweetened cream to the yogurt and whisk thoroughly.

In a large measuring cup, dissolve the sodium alginate into the water using a stick blender. Let rest for 30 minutes until the liquid is clear. Using a child's medicine dosing spoon, drop yolk-sized dollops of cream into the sodium alginate bath. Gently coax the sphere around to ensure that it is coated with the slimy sodium alginate liquid. Leave in the bath for 30 seconds, then remove to a second container filled with plain water. Hold the spheres in the water until ready to serve, being sure not to overcrowd the holding water—leaving enough space for you to insert a spoon to pick up the spheres.

MAKE SWEET CORN DUKKAH:

Place the corn and seeds in a small skillet and toast until fragrant. Transfer the toasted ingredients and the black pepper and salt to a small food processor and grind into a coarse powder. Hold in an airtight container until ready to serve.

To serve, make a nest of beet strips on the plate, leaving a 1-inch clear circle in the center. Gently lay the yogurt sphere in the center of the nest and top with microgreens, a sprinkle of dukkah, and maple flakes. (Tonewood sells maple flakes—see Resources.)

CAULIFLOWER BLACK MOLE

Black mole, or mole negro, is something I always wanted to like as a kid, but I could never get past the bitter taste and pasty consistency of the store-bought moles. But besides having to gather a lot of ingredients, mole is not that difficult to make, and now I have a mole that I love. This recipe is for the restaurant's popular cauliflower, but you can just as easily serve it over chicken with cilantro rice.

BLACK MOLE

10 Oaxacan black chiles, dried
10 guajillo chiles, dried
6 pasilla chiles, dried
6 ancho chiles, dried
6 New Mexico red chiles, dried
320 g (2 cups) onion, chopped
65 g (½ cup) garlic cloves, chopped
65 g (½ cup) almonds, chopped
2-inch cinnamon stick, broken into small pieces
1 tbsp peppercorns
1 tbsp cloves
65 ml (¼ cup) neutral cooking oil, such as canola
50 g (¼ cup) neutral cooking oil
40 g (¼ cup) raisins
50 g (2 cups) brioche, challah, or other rich egg bread, torn
1 green banana, peeled
65 g (½ cup) sesame seeds
240 g (1½ cups) tomatoes, chopped
80 g (½ cup) tomatillos, chopped
1 sprig fresh thyme
1 sprig fresh oregano
2 abuelita Mexican chocolate discs
salt, to taste

ROASTED MOLE CAULIFLOWER

neutral cooking oil
2 cauliflower heads
575 g (2 cups) Black Mole

MAKE BLACK MOLE:

Remove the stems and seeds from the chiles and toast chiles in dry skillet until smoky. Boil a small stockpot of water and add the toasted, dried chiles. Submerge the chiles, cover, and let soak for 30 minutes. Note that if you can't find these specific chiles, use what you can get at your store. You are looking for a variety of dried large chiles.

Combine the onion, garlic, almonds, cinnamon, peppercorns, and cloves in a skillet and sauté until the onion softens. Put the mixture in a blender with 1 cup of the chile water and all of the soaked chiles. Blend until smooth, adding the chile water as necessary to allow the mixture to flow in the blender.

In a large stockpot, melt the neutral cooking oil over medium heat. Add chile mixture and sauté 5 minutes. Add the remaining ingredients, along with the remaining chile water. Reduce heat to a simmer and continue simmering for no less than 1 hour and ideally 3 or more hours, stirring regularly. You now have mole negro (Black Mole) that you can use with chicken, shrimp, or this cauliflower dish.

MAKE ROASTED MOLE CAULIFLOWER:

Preheat the oven to 450°F.

Coat the bottom of a heavy-duty baking sheet with neutral cooking oil. Cut the cauliflower into ½-inch slices, trying your best to keep the slices intact, although they will inevitably crumble. Lay the slices in a single layer across the pan. Coat with more oil—be generous, not healthy! Bake for 20 minutes. Turn the pieces of cauliflower over (this is why we try to keep it in big pieces) and bake an additional 20 minutes. Turn one more time and continue cooking until the cauliflower becomes dark brown. Near the end, brush the Black Mole generously over the cauliflower and return to the oven for 5 more minutes. Lightly salt and serve.

> **SUGGESTED SUBSTITUTIONS:** You can mix and match chiles to create your own flavor; however, if you don't have black chiles, you won't have black mole.

GINGER HOREHOUND COOKIES

Make no mistakes about it—horehound is bitter. Many foraged ingredient beer brewers use it as a bittering agent in place of hops. Here, we use it to balance out the deep sweetness of molasses, and it plays curiously with the biting fresh ginger. These cookies are one of my favorite hiking snacks, and in fact, they can be found in crumb form at the bottom of most of my jacket pockets right now.

765 g (6 cups) all-purpose flour
4 tsp baking soda
½ tsp salt
336 g (1½ cups) unsalted butter
110 g (½ cup) sugar
320 g (1½ cups) brown sugar
3 tbsp dried horehound, ground (p. 204)
2 inches fresh ginger, grated
40 g (¼ cup) candied ginger, minced
1 tsp cinnamon, freshly grated
½ tsp cloves, freshly ground
2 eggs, room temperature
160 g (½ cup) molasses

Combine the flour, soda, and salt in a bowl. In the bowl of a stand mixer fitted with the paddle attachment, beat the butter and sugars until light and fluffy. Add the horehound, gingers, cinnamon, and cloves, and whip until spices are consistently spread throughout the butter. Add the eggs one at a time, and then the molasses. Turn the mixer to low and add the dry ingredients, mixing just until they come together—do not overmix! Scoop the dough with an ice cream scoop onto a parchment paper–lined tray and chill for at least an hour. Roll the dough balls in sugar and bake at 350°F for 25 minutes.

CACTUS CAKE WITH YUCCA BLOSSOM JAM

People love to challenge me to odd cooking. One challenge I accepted was to create a dessert using all of the local cacti. The result captures the natural citrus sweetness that permeates cactus fruit. These fruit are abundant, healthy, and really tasty. Plenty of substitutions make this doable all across North America.

YUCCA BLOSSOM JAM

125 g (4 cups) fresh yucca blossom petals, cleaned (p. 37)
125 g (½ cup) sugar, divided
250 ml (1 cup) water
2 tbsp lemon juice
Mesquite Sumac Shortbread dough (p. 160)

PRICKLY PEAR BAVAROISE

340 g (1¼ cups) goat cheese
65 ml (¼ cup) agave nectar
2 sheets silver gelatin (2 tsp powdered), softened
58 g (¼ cup) cream cheese
115 g (½ cup) crème fraiche (or sour cream)
55 g (¼ cup) sugar
85 ml (⅓ cup) prickly pear juice (p. 35)
375 ml (1½ cups) heavy cream

MAKE YUCCA BLOSSOM JAM:

Carefully clean the petals, making sure that they are free of dirt and bugs. Sprinkle a quarter of the sugar over the petals and massage the sugar into the petals with your hands. Once bruised, the petals offer a light green scent that remind you of unripe melon rind. Place in bowl, wrap with plastic wrap, and let rest in the fridge overnight.

In a saucepan, combine the remaining sugar, the water, and the juice and cook on medium heat, stirring occasionally. Just as the mixture comes to a simmer, add the sugared petals and their remaining sugar to the pan. Gently simmer for 5 minutes. Raise the heat and boil for about 20 minutes or until the mixture starts to thicken. I prefer to leave it slightly runny. The jam can be used as soon as it cools or canned for gifts and preserving.

Roll out the Mesquite Sumac Shortbread dough to ⅛-inch thickness. Cut to fit the interior of the cake mold. Freeze and bake as per the recipe. Trim the shortbread as needed to ensure that the cookie fits inside the cake mold.

MAKE PRICKLY PEAR BAVAROISE:

In the bowl of a double boiler, warm the goat cheese, agave nectar, gelatin, and cream cheese, and slowly stir until smooth and creamy. Remove from the heat and add the crème fraiche, sugar, and juice. Whisk to combine. Whip cream to soft peaks and fold the cheese mixture into the cream. Pipe into the desired mold, set the Mesquite Sumac Shortbread into the bavaroise (the top of the bavaroise will become the bottom of the cake when released from the mold), and freeze overnight.

To serve, remove the cake from the mold at least 1 hour before serving, allowing it to thaw in the refrigerator. Serve with the Yucca Blossom Jam. For added flair, sprinkle local bee pollen, spin caramelized sugar, and roughly chop into sugar needles. You can coat the cake with these needles to create your "cactus."

ALMOND OLIVE TEACAKE

I don't tell people what's in this cake, letting them think the dark specks are chocolate chips. But olives, orange, and almonds are a perfect combination and, worked into this afternoon teacake, their flavors will shine through. Russian olives are similar in size to capers and can be found throughout much of the United States.

CURED RUSSIAN OLIVES
160 g (1 cup) Russian olives (p. 205)
120 g (½ cup) salt

ALMOND CAKE
225 g (2½ cups) almond meal
1 tsp baking powder
110 g (½ cup) sugar, divided
4 eggs, separated
zest of 2 oranges
1 tsp salt
80 g (½ cup) cured Russian olives (p. 205)
2 tbsp amontillado sherry
1 tbsp orange blossom water

MAKE CURED RUSSIAN OLIVES:

Toss the olives and salt together in an airtight container and let sit for 4 hours. Run the olives through a sifter to remove the salt, and then rinse to remove any remaining salt.

MAKE ALMOND CAKE:

Preheat the oven to 375°F.

Butter a 9-inch springform pan and line with parchment paper. Whisk the almond meal, baking powder, and roughly one-third of the sugar in a bowl. In a separate bowl, whisk the yolks and the second third of the sugar until light in color. Add the zest, salt, and olives to the yolks and whisk a few more minutes. Add the sherry and orange blossom water to the yolk mixture and whisk to combine. Pour the yolk mixture into the almond meal and, using a rubber spatula, fold until thoroughly combined.

In the bowl of a stand mixer fitted with the whisk attachment, whisk the egg whites until soft peaks form. Add the final third of the sugar and whisk until medium peaks are formed—don't allow the whites to become stiff, or the cake will be dry and crumbly. Fold a third of the whites into the almond meal mixture, and then gently fold the remaining whites, creating a smooth batter. Stop folding as soon as the mixture is homogenous; otherwise, your cake will deflate during baking.

Bake 30 minutes or until firm to the touch and an inserted toothpick comes out clean.

> **SUGGESTED SUBSTITUTIONS:** Replace the foraged Russian olives with kalamata olives chopped into small pieces.

CARROT SPICE CAKE

Our local farmers love to grow carrots for me, and I'm never one to refuse anything that is brought to me, so I occasionally end up with too many carrots. I decided it was time to transform the antiquated carrot cake into this stunning pastry.

LEMON CURD

500 ml (2 cups) lemon juice
225 g (1 cup) unsalted butter
6 egg yolks
6 eggs
110 g (½ cup) sugar
2 sheets silver gelatin (2 tsp powder), softened

SPICE CAKE

128 g (1 cup) bread flour
128 g (1 cup) cake flour
1 tsp salt
1 tbsp ground ginger
1 tbsp ground sumac
1 tsp cinnamon, ground
1 tsp cloves, crushed
½ tsp nutmeg, grated
9 eggs, room temperature
220 g (1 cup) muscovado sugar

CARROT MOUSSE

4 carrots, peeled, chopped
65 ml (¼ cup) lemon juice
55 g (¼ cup) sugar
4 sheets silver gelatin (4 tsp powder), softened
2 tbsp brandy
375 ml (1½ cups) cream

CARAMEL GLAZE

1 tsp salt
3 tbsp water
30 g (¼ cup) cornstarch
440 g (2 cups) sugar
125 ml (½ cup) water
375 ml (1½ cups) cream
4 sheets silver gelatin (4 tsp powder), softened

MAKE LEMON CURD:

Heat juice and butter in a saucepan until the butter is melted and simmering. In a mixing bowl, whisk the yolks, eggs, and sugar until lightened in color. Pour a quarter of the hot juice into the eggs, whisking constantly, and then return the mixture to the remaining hot juice. Cook on low, stirring constantly, until slightly thickened. Remove from the heat and add the gelatin. Pour the curd onto a rimmed baking sheet lined with plastic wrap. Allow to set until firm in the refrigerator.

MAKE SPICE CAKE:

Preheat the oven to 325°F.

Line a rimmed sheet pan with parchment paper and then butter the parchment. Whisk the flours, salt, and spices together in a bowl. In a stand mixer fitted with the whisk attachment, whip the eggs and sugar on high until a ribbon of batter falls from the whisk. Carefully fold the dry ingredients into the egg mixture and pour into the lined pan. Bake 15 minutes or until set. Let cool to room temperature.

MAKE CARROT MOUSSE:

Cook the carrots and lemon juice in a covered saucepan until soft. Add the sugar and cook, uncovered, for an additional 2 minutes. Cool to room temperature. Add the gelatin and brandy and process in a blender until smooth. Strain the purée and hold. Whip the cream to soft peaks and fold the carrot mixture into the cream. Pipe into your mold and freeze.

MAKE CARAMEL GLAZE:

In a small bowl, combine the salt, 3 tablespoons water, and cornstarch. In a large saucepan, over medium heat, combine the sugar and ½ cup water. Cook the sugar slurry until it caramelizes and reaches 338°F. In the meantime, heat the cream until hot. Carefully pour the hot cream into the caramel and whisk until all the caramel has dissolved. Add the cornstarch mixture to the caramel sauce and cook until thickened, about 5 minutes. Remove the pan from heat and let sit for 5 minutes. Add the gelatin and cool to room temperature.

Remove the carrot mousse from the freezer and take out of the mold cavities. Set the mousses on a drying rack and smoothly pour the caramel glaze on top. Transfer the glazed mousses to a sheet and let thaw in the refrigerator for at least 1 hour.

To serve, plate the glazed mousse, cake, and curd. You can also add foraged wood sorrel and candied nuts.

PEANUT BUTTER PIE

I've loved peanut butter pie ever since my time in New Orleans, but often, it either doesn't taste peanut buttery enough for me or the recipe includes cream cheese, which doesn't seem right to my tastes. I worked for years to create this perfect pie!

150 g (1 cup) peanuts, shelled, unroasted

65 ml (¼ cup) LeBlanc roasted peanut oil, plus more as needed*

2 tbsp honey

500 ml (2 cups) milk

147 g (⅔ cup) sugar

30 g (¼ cup) cornstarch

1 tsp salt

4 egg yolks

2 tbsp unsalted butter

128 g (½ cup) creamy peanut butter

125 ml (½ cup) cream

Place the peanuts in a 300°F oven, and toast them until dark brown and fragrant. Transfer the nuts to a food processor and grind. As the pieces get about the size of coarse sand, add the oil and continue processing until a thick paste is achieved. You may need to adjust the amount of oil depending on the freshness of your peanuts. Add the honey and you have your own homemade peanut butter.

In a bowl, microwave the milk for 5 minutes or until simmering. While heating, whisk the sugar, cornstarch, and salt in a mixing bowl. Add the yolks to the sugar mixture and whisk—it will be thick. Pour a third of the hot milk into the sugar-yolk slurry and whisk until smooth. Return the yolk mixture to the hot milk and whisk again. Microwave for 60 seconds and then whisk. At this point, continue microwaving in 30-second blasts, followed by whisking, until the mixture is thickened like a loose pudding.

Add the peanut butter and whisk to combine. Pour into a new bowl and cover with plastic wrap to prevent a skin from forming. Cool in the fridge until the mixture reaches room temperature—not chilled. Whip the cream to soft peaks and fold into the peanut butter pudding. Serve in pie shells or in a cup. I fill a pastry bag and squirt it directly into my mouth. (Voila! A gluten-free pie.) Top with caramelized Puffed Amaranth (p. 166).

*NOTE: LeBlanc nut oils are truly the best I've ever found. This French company hasn't let me down in nearly a decade with their pure and bold flavors. If you don't want to make your own peanut butter, replace with ½ cup of storebought peanut butter. Jif is known to be the most peanut buttery of the different brands.

SWEET CORN SUMAC BONBONS

For a short time, there was a trend emerging of dipping corn tortilla chips into chocolate. It grew enough that a few national snack makers even tried their hands at it. While the textures never quite worked, the flavors do, and that led me to create this bonbon.

See chocolate tempering instructions on p. 85.

85 ml (⅓ cup) cream + more as needed

163 g (1½ cups) freshly cut corn kernels, plus the stripped cobs

70 g (½ cup) sumac berries (p. 36)

1½ tbsp corn syrup

225 g (1½ cups) white chocolate, chopped

2 tbsp butter

1 tbsp cayenne pepper

Bring cream, kernels, cobs, sumac, and corn syrup to a simmer for 2 minutes. Remove from heat and let rest, covered, for 30 minutes. Strain the cream and top off with additional cream to return to the total weight of 150 grams. Return the cream to a simmer. Place the white chocolate in a food processor and grind to small pebbles. Slowly pour the hot cream over the ground chocolate and let rest a few minutes, then process until smooth; add the butter and cayenne, processing a bit more until no butter shows. Transfer ganache to a piping bag. Pipe into prepared chocolate molds and let set overnight. Spread a thin layer of tempered chocolate onto the bottom of the molds to cap the bonbons; allow to set firm, and serve.

CARAMEL AMARANTH BONBONS

Caramel fillings are always popular with my customers. But often caramel becomes too rich. That's why there's been an explosion of "salted caramel." The salt cuts the richness. Here, I go a different route by adding some earthiness and texture to the rich, creamy caramel.

125 ml (½ cup) brown ale beer (we use whatever beer we are currently brewing in house)

125 ml (½ cup) cream

37 g (½ cup) amaranth seeds, lightly toasted (p. 166)

peel of 1 orange

20 g (1 cup) four-wing saltbush leaves (p. 191)

110 g (½ cup) sugar

2 tbsp corn syrup

150 g (1 cup) milk chocolate chips (see chocolate tempering instructions on p. 85)

Combine beer, cream, amaranth, orange peel, and leaves in a medium saucepan. Bring to a simmer for 2 minutes. Hold, covered, to keep warm. In a stainless steel or copper pan, melt the sugar and corn syrup over medium-high heat. Stir very gently as the sugar begins to caramelize. Cook to a light golden brown. Carefully strain the hot beer cream into the caramel. Whisk gently until a creamy, loose caramel sauce is obtained. Let rest covered for 5 minutes.

Grind the chocolate in a food processor until small pebbles are formed. Pour the beer cream over the chocolate and process until smooth. Transfer to a piping bag and fill the chocolate molds, allowing them to set up overnight. Spread a thin layer of tempered chocolate onto the bottom of the molds to cap the bonbons; allow to set firm, and serve.

VIETNAMESE COFFEE BOMB

I call these bombs because eager eaters like me will put the whole thing in their mouth at once and have the shell explode, giving way to the rich coffee filling. Just be warned that there is always one dainty diner who will try to nibble at the sphere, which will inevitably burst and cover their clean white shirt with a dark brown stain.

65 ml (¼ cup) sweetened condensed milk

1 egg yolk

375 ml (1½ cups) coffee, freshly brewed, hot and strong

300 g (2 cups) 65% chocolate, melted and tempered (see instructions on p. 85)

Whisk the sweetened condensed milk and yolk together in a small bowl. Pour a quarter of the hot coffee into the mixture and whisk until combined. Return the hot yolk mixture to the remaining coffee and cook in a saucepan over a medium heat, stirring constantly, until thickened. Remove from the heat and pipe into 1-inch sphere molds. Freeze overnight.

To serve, poke the coffee ball with a toothpick and dip in the tempered chocolate. The frozen coffee will set the chocolate shell rather quickly. Place the sphere on a parchment paper–lined tray and fill the hole from the toothpick with a spot of chocolate to seal the sphere. Let thaw in the refrigerator for at least 1 hour, watching for leaks.

PRICKLY PEAR MARGARITA PÂTÉ DE FRUIT

The beautiful magenta color will draw them in like flies, but the smack of tequila will swat them down!

   30

190 ml (¾ cup) prickly pear juice
    (p. 35)
2 tbsp lemon juice
125 ml (½ cup) tequila
440 g (2 cups) sugar, divided
10 g (4 tsp) yellow pectin
75 g (½ cup + 2 tbsp) glucose
    powder
cooking oil
1 tbsp citric acid
1 tbsp tequila
sugar, for finishing

In a large saucepan, warm juices and the ½ cup tequila to 104°F. In a small bowl, whisk ¼ cup of the sugar and pectin together. Pour the remaining of sugar and glucose in a second bowl. When the juices and tequila hit 104°F, add the sugar-pectin mixture and whisk, ensuring no lumps form. Bring to a boil. Add the sugar and glucose mixture to the juices and tequila and cook to 223°F, stirring. While the mixture is cooking, prepare your frames or molds by brushing them lightly with oil.

When the mixture reaches 223°F, remove from the heat and pour in the citric acid and the 1 tablespoon tequila. Whisk quickly and pour the mixture into the prepared mold. Let set at room temperature until firm to the touch. Cut, toss in sugar, and serve.

SUMAC SHANDY

We brew our own beer at the restaurant, and we like to do a "dry hop" technique using three-leaf sumac. At home, I recommend mixing sumac tea into your bought beer. Please be sure to use the correct sumac (*Rhus trilobata*) and not the common eastern poison sumac (*Toxicodendron vernix*), or you'll be in for a rough night of drinking!

144 g (1 cup) sumac berries (p. 36)
55 g (¼ cup) sugar
500 ml (2 cups) water

Place berries and sugar in a saucepan with the water and bring to a gentle simmer. Cover and simmer for 15 more minutes. Remove from heat and let steep for 30 minutes. Strain berries out of the liquid and cool the tea to room temperature. Add ¼ cup of sumac tea for every 12 ounces of beer.

4 | FROM THE FIELD (WILD PLANTS)

FUNGUS, FRESHNESS & FOUL PLAY

I've come to accept that mistakes and lessons learned are part of my foraging experience.

A year ago, I stumbled upon nearly twenty-five pounds of oyster mushrooms. I had never looked for mushrooms in this particular area before, but my gut said to search through the downed trees and sure enough—the mother lode!

My standard for oyster mushrooms is never to remove more than half of the bounty on the tree—essentially leaving the base for future growth. When I returned to the same spot one month later to chart the tree's location for future foraging, the remainder of the mushrooms was gone, clearly chopped off by human hands. I was furious! How could someone ruin the likelihood of an ongoing harvest?

Once I cooled down, I realized that another forager simply saw an oyster mushroom . . . not a mushroom that I had already foraged. So the later forager took his or her portion . . . and perhaps a series of people took their portions. Regardless of how it played out, the damage was done. I now take laminated cards that announce that I harvested and an explanation of how oyster mushrooms replenish in hopes that subsequent foragers will respect nature's cycle.

On my most recent visit to that same tree, there was not even a sign of any oyster mushroom growth—the colony was dead.

Each and every foraging moment is full of ethical, philosophical, and biological choices. Being aware of these choices will allow you and other foragers to have a lifetime of discovery and great meals. Ignoring those choices will lead to empty baskets.

PROFILE: RICHARD FELGER:
"Bringing Local Plants Back"

by Andrea Feucht

Mesquite. It's a flavor, right? One of those savory or once-trendy flavors found in potato chips or charcoal or bacon. To most of us—even to me until recently—mesquite is only a flavoring ingredient. But what we think of as "mesquite" flavor is what remains in the smoky aroma after burning mesquite wood. In the desert Southwest, however, mesquite as a fully utilized plant has a history of cultural significance deeper than many people realize. This plant has served almost as a foundation to entire native cultures—the Pima of Arizona are but one. Mesquite can be food, fiber, lumber, firewood, soil stabilizer, and drought survivor.

This brings us to Richard Felger, one of a handful of experts leading modern research about mesquite (along with other traditional native plants)—specifically about how mesquite might be one of the old crops our new drought-pummeled culture needs. For now, Richard sits at the patio table, brow scrunching as he squints in the noon light, an olive-green work shirt draped over his shoulders with familial softness. Age seems to be struggling to keep up with his physical stature; what looks like "sixty-ish" is actually over seventy. This means he's been a biology professional for half a century. In that time, he has published more than a hundred research papers and dozens of articles, and in the last decade his focus is all about food sustainability. His enthusiasm is muted but percolates in his eyes as he talks about what amazing resources the desert can provide humans.

Richard is an associate researcher with the University of Arizona Herbarium, just over the state line from New Mexico, but he calls the outskirts of Silver City home. Without any doubt, he has always been a scientist. There's a point in our conversation when he talks about his young interest in the life sciences; he mentions that he started out as a marine biologist but changed course and decided botany was his calling. This was at age eight. Richard's face betrays no smirk, no punchline: he's dead serious. And that's what comes through when you speak with him about anything in his work. He's not overly formal or somber about the profession he chose in his childhood—just earnest and collected in a manner that has come from decades of fastidious work.

Rob and Richard met when Rob started thinking about using plants that could be cultivated in or around Silver City. Rob was (and is) always looking to add to his knowledge of foraging. Using locally sustainable and recognizable crops like piñon are of interest when you would like to entice diners into trying new flavors. Bringing in underappreciated plants is also key when promoting the sustainability of something the desert provides.

When you ask Richard which plants a modernist forage-oriented restaurant like Rob's could put to good use—that is, which plants are easy to grow and harvest and which have culinary utility—he will say that several come to mind. First, there are two grasses that can be easily found (or deliberately grown) in the Southwest: bulb panicgrass and big alkali sacaton. Both are drought-hardy with highly nutritious seeds, though the seeds from the sacaton are easier to harvest. Next are plants in the daisy family that already proliferate in Silver City and are candidates for incorporation into Rob's cooking: wild tarragon (the leaves as well as the seeds) and goldeneye, with its tiny sunflower-like seeds.

When Rob holds experimental dinners, he's doing what he loves best *and* he's preaching to the choir: everyone at those events endorses foraging and strange, new ingredients. But it is on Rob's everyday menu—with his regular local customers—that he can make converts, such as including mesquite flour in baked goods, using wild amaranth in a salad, and so on. This means The Curious Kumquat is using knowledge from people like Richard to impact both sets of foodies. Each type of cooking serves a purpose and an audience. That's how Rob educates and expands the palates of modern diners.

WILD GRASS RISOTTO

At the restaurant, we work with Richard Felger (p. 140), who is a renowned researcher on food sustainability in arid environments; specifically, he's a grass expert. Apaches have long eaten grass seed, typically in the form of gruel or porridge. My role in working with Richard is to bring this historic food source into the modern era, making it more palatable. One of my favorite uses is as risotto, which offers ample protein and texture to a meal.

1 liter (4½ cups) Rabbit Stock (p. 98)
4 tbsp butter
80 g (½ cup) onion, finely chopped
200 g (1 cup) farro grain
40 g (½ cup) wild grass seed*, winnowed**
250 ml (1 cup) riesling wine, room temperature
salt and pepper, to taste
2 tbsp cattail pollen (p. 33)

Heat the stock in a saucepan to a simmer and hold.

In a large sauté pan, melt the butter over medium heat. Once the butter is melted, add the onion and cook until translucent. Add the farro grain and cook until toasty brown and fragrant. Add the grass seed to the pan and toast another 2 minutes. Grass seed toasts very quickly compared to the farro grain, so less time is needed. Be prepared for popping seeds.

Add the hot stock 1 cup at a time, stirring gently until almost absorbed. Continue adding the stock ½ cup at a time. Depending on the farro, you may not add all the broth, or you may need to add some water. Simply cook to your texture preference—we like al dente, soft with a little chew. After the stock has all been incorporated, pour the wine in the pan and reduce it until only a thin layer remains. Add salt and pepper to taste. Finally, add the cattail pollen for a burst of color and a sweet umami background. You can serve with braised rabbit or a delicate chicken breast.

*NOTE: Consult your local extension office for indigenous edible grasses in your area. We focus on bulb panicgrass (*Panicum bulbosum*) and Nash giant dropseed (*Sporobolus giganteus*), both of which are high-level producers that are easily found.

**NOTE: Winnowing grass seed is not a fun day in our kitchen. If you're not up for a *Little House on the Prairie* moment, you can easily substitute by purchasing amaranth seed at your local health food store or online.

> **SUGGESTED SUBSTITUTIONS:** Amaranth can be used in the same quantity as the grass seed. If cattail pollen is unavailable, you can take the recipe in a different direction by replacing with 1 teaspoon of saffron. You can substitute chicken stock for rabbit stock if you prefer.

CATTAIL HUMMUS WITH STINGING NETTLE SAUCE

Who doesn't like to eat something called "Stinging Nettle Sauce?" Over the years, I've learned to enjoy nature's pain when I've foraged. I'll pop cactus fruit straight in my mouth only to endure the numb and tingling sensations on my tongue from the needles a week after. Stinging nettles offer the same hazard. Roll the leaves into themselves, rolling toward the underside of the leaf, then pop them in your mouth. The leaves hold a strong chlorophyll flavor with hints of pepper, citrus, and maybe even a bit of bitter chocolate. The price you pay—a numb tongue, but it's only a temporary price! In the restaurant, we're sure to blanch and shock the leaves to remove the sting and bring out that bold, beautiful flavor before serving it to customers.

CATTAIL HUMMUS

350 g (2 cups) cattail stalk, outer woody material removed (p. 33)
2 tbsp white miso
2 tbsp lime juice
1 tsp sumac, dried (p. 36)
salt, to taste

JUNIPER MELON

1 locally raised melon, such as cantaloupe
6 juniper berries, crushed

STINGING NETTLE SAUCE

50 g (1 cup) stinging nettle leaves
salt, to taste
0.3 g (⅛ tsp) xanthan gum

SESAME OIL POWDER

20 g (1 cup) tapioca maltodextrin
3 tbsp toasted sesame seed oil
1 tsp salt

SUGGESTED SUBSTITUTIONS:

If you don't have fresh cattail, we've also made this dish using cucumber. Reduce the lime juice by half to lower the liquid content. If stinging nettles are not available, you can substitute spinach or arugula leaves.

MAKE CATTAIL HUMMUS:

Place all of the hummus ingredients in a food processor and process until smooth, leaving just a bit of texture. Store covered in the refrigerator until ready to serve.

MAKE JUNIPER MELON:

Using a large melon baller, make a number of melon balls. Place the melon balls and juniper berries into a vacuum bag and seal. Let rest in the refrigerator overnight. Remove the balls and discard the juniper berries. Hold the melon balls chilled until ready to serve.

MAKE STINGING NETTLE SAUCE:

Fill a small saucepan with water and bring to a boil. Fill a small bowl with ice and water. Add the nettle leaves to the boiling water and boil for 15 seconds. Quickly remove the leaves and shock in the ice water. If you cook the leaves longer than 15 seconds, you end up with slime. What you want is a vibrant green color and a remarkable nettle flavor. Cool the boiling liquid to room temperature.

Place the leaves in a blender, and with the blender running, add 1 cup of the cooled boiling liquid to create a bright green liquid whirlpool. Salt to taste. With the blender still running, add the xanthan gum and transfer to a squirt bottle. Chill.

MAKE SESAME OIL POWDER:

Gently pour the tapioca maltodextrin in a large mixing bowl, being careful not to create a cloud of powder that you really don't want in your lungs. Slowly whisk the powder while drizzling in the oil. Whisk more aggressively as the oil adheres to the powder, until a light lumpy snow is formed. Sprinkle the salt into the powder and whisk again. Store in an airtight container until ready to serve.

Pipe the hummus onto the serving plate. Add microgreens and paper-thin sliced carrots. Add the Juniper Melon, stinging nettle sauce with sesame seed oil powder, and grate sweet juniper berry on the top and add a squirt of the stinging nettle sauce.

CATTAIL SALAD

This salad is inspired by the classic Green Papaya salad. Cattails lend themselves to this dish by bringing juicy, crisp flesh that pairs well with the bold flavors of Thai dressing. It's fast, it's easy, and it will always please your guests.

1 ripe mango, peeled, diced
6 (6-inch) stalks cattail, peeled of outer woody material, julienned (p. 33)
3 tbsp shallot, minced
2 tbsp shredded coconut
2 tbsp Thai basil, julienned
2 tbsp mint, julienned
1 tbsp roasted Thai chile, crushed
2 tbsp fish sauce
2 tbsp lime juice

Combine all the ingredients in a bowl and chill for 30 minutes to allow flavors to marry. You can store the salad for a day but no more; after that, the cattail will start to break down and become slimy. A half hour rest is ideal.

SUGGESTED SUBSTITUTIONS: If you don't have cattail, use green papaya.

ACORN PASTA WITH SPICY CRAWFISH

In those instances when I have totally forgotten to prepare a dish for a special event, I kick into autopilot and, within minutes, my time in New Orleans shines through. This was such a dish. I had been playing around with preserving kumquats similarly to preserving lemons, and at the same time I was using up last season's acorn flour. The result was this Cajun-inspired flavor giant! Enjoy with an Abita beer and some Dr. John blasting out of your iPod.

PRESERVED KUMQUATS

100 g (1 cup) kumquats
50 g (¼ cup) salt
50 g (¼ cup) sugar
1 cinnamon stick
1 star anise
125 ml (½ cup) lemon juice

ACORN PASTA

42 g (⅓ cup) tapioca flour
38 g (⅓ cup) acorn flour (p. 31)
42 g (⅓ cup) all-purpose flour
½ tsp salt
1 tbsp neutral cooking oil, such as canola
90 ml (¼ cup + 2 tbsp) water, plus more as needed

SPICY CRAWFISH SAUCE

¼ cup neutral cooking oil, such as canola
32 g (¼ cup) all-purpose flour
160 g (1 cup) onion, chopped
160 g (1 cup) red bell pepper, chopped
160 g (1 cup) celery, chopped
1 tbsp fresh oregano
1 tsp fresh thyme
1 tbsp black pepper, freshly ground
500 ml (2 cups) cream
400 g (2 cups) crawfish, shelled & deveined
2 tbsp cayenne pepper
salt, to taste

MAKE PRESERVED KUMQUATS:

Cut kumquats in half lengthwise. In a mixing bowl, toss the kumquats with the salt and sugar. Let rest for 1 hour at room temperature. Stuff the kumquats into a sterile canning jar, scraping the sugar and salt onto the top. Add the cinnamon and anise and top the jar with lemon juice. Let stand for a minimum of 48 hours and up to a week.

MAKE ACORN PASTA:

Combine the three flours and salt in a stand mixer fitted with the paddle attachment. With the paddle running, drizzle the oil and water into the flours. It is inevitable that you will need to add more water to achieve a firm but not hard dough. Remove the dough from the bowl and knead by hand on the counter for an additional 10 minutes or until the dough is smooth. Add water or flour as necessary. The dough should be pliable but not sticky.

Wrap the dough in plastic wrap and let rest for 1 hour at room temperature.

When you are ready to use the pasta, cut a golf ball–sized chunk, press it with the heel of your hand, and roll out with your pasta roller or rolling pin to ⅛-inch thickness. Cut the pasta to your desired shape. Let rest on a drying rack until it's time to boil.

MAKE SPICY CRAWFISH SAUCE:

In a large saucepan, heat the oil over medium-high heat until shimmering. Add the flour and stir constantly until it turns a medium chestnut brown. You've just made a beautiful roux. Immediately add the onion, pepper, and celery. Stir to coat with the roux. Cook for 5 minutes or until the vegetables turn slightly soft. Add all the herbs and pepper and cook until fragrant. Pour the cream into the pan and combine, bringing to a simmer. Add the crawfish and stir. Maintain a simmer and cook until the crawfish are done (10 to 15 minutes), seasoning with salt and cayenne prior to serving.

Cook the pasta in salted boiling water for 8 to 10 minutes or until al dente. Chop the Preserved Kumquats and add them to the Spicy Crawfish Sauce. Pour over the pasta.

SUGGESTED SUBSTITUTIONS: Substitute whole wheat flour or an ultra fine nut powder if you don't have acorns. Crawfish are often available in the freezer aisle of the grocery store or in Asian markets, but if not, substitute shrimp.

PURPLE POTATO GNOCCHI WITH HOUSE-CURED HAM

Start this recipe today, because it won't be ready for a few years! There is such a satisfaction in having the patience to create food that takes months or years. Yes, you can simply buy dry-cured ham at the grocery, but the reward for doing it yourself is something that is truly irreplaceable.

HOUSE CURED HAM

908 g (4 lb) kosher salt
fresh pork leg, with skin
410 g (2 cups) lard, plus more as needed
white peppercorns
dried hackberries (p. 34)

PARMESAN SAUCE

227 g (½ lb) parmesan cheese
500 ml (2 cups) cream
salt, to taste
4 g (1 tsp) xanthan gum

PURPLE POTATO GNOCCHI

454 g (1 lb) purple potatoes
65 g (½ cup) all-purpose flour, divided
1 tsp salt

MAKE HOUSE-CURED HAM:

Aggressively rub the salt all over the pork leg, being sure to coat the entire surface. Place the pork leg in a large plastic tub and cover. Store in the refrigerator. Every day, look at the ham and make sure that salt is covering the entire surface—you may notice uneven discoloration, which is a sign that you missed a spot. Wear gloves to keep the environment sanitary and free of unwanted bacteria. As the ham ages, pour off excess moisture and add salt as necessary. The curing is complete when the ham is firm to the touch, but plan on 1 day for each pound of meat.

Once firm, wipe the salt from the ham and rinse under a faucet with extremely clean hands. Pat the ham completely dry with paper towels. With gloved hands, coat the ham with the lard and toss the peppercorns and hackberries all over the surface, pressing them into the lard.

Hang the ham in a meat cellar or wine cooler at 55–60°F for 18 months. During that time, watch diligently for mold formation or meat that is exposed and drying. If you find it, simply scrape the old lard away and apply new lard, always being conscious of cleanliness.

(To save time, simply buy prosciutto ham at the grocery store.)

MAKE PARMESAN SAUCE:

To make the sauce, chop the cheese into ½-inch cubes. Place in a medium saucepan with the cream. Reduce the heat to low and let cook for 30 minutes or until the cheese is soft; it will maintain its shape but will become soft. Stir the cheese from time to time to prevent sticking. Using an immersion blender, combine the soft cheese and cream. Taste for saltiness and adjust as desired. Add the xanthan gum and blend again until homogenous and slightly thick. Hold at room temperature until ready to serve.

MAKE PURPLE POTATO GNOCCHI:

Bake the potatoes with the skin on, wrapped in foil, for approximately 60 minutes or until soft when poked with a fork. Cut the potatoes in half lengthwise and scrape the filling out with a spoon. Place the potatoes in a large bowl and add half the flour. Using a fork, cut the flour into the potato. Add the remaining flour and salt a little at a time, again cutting in with a fork, until a Play-Doh-like consistency is formed. Shape into a rough square and pat down to 1-inch thickness.

Working on a very lightly floured surface, cut the square into 1-inch wide strips. Roll the strips into ropes that end up being ½-inch thick. Cut the ropes into 1-inch lengths. Let the gnocchi air dry for at least 30 minutes.

HAZELNUT OIL PUDDING

250 ml (1 cup) milk
2 egg yolks
73 g (⅓ cup) sugar
3 tbsp cornstarch
1 tsp salt
3 tbsp roasted hazelnut oil
     (we prefer LeBlanc oils)

MAKE HAZELNUT OIL PUDDING:

Heat milk in a saucepan over medium heat. Meanwhile, combine yolks, sugar, cornstarch, and salt in a mixing bowl and whisk to combine. When milk comes to a simmer, pour a third of it into the yolk mixture, whisking constantly. Return the hot yolk mixture to the remaining milk and whisk. Return to the heat and cook, stirring constantly, until slightly thickened. Drizzle hazelnut oil into the pudding while whisking and continue until homogenous.

To serve, bring a pot of salted water to a soft boil. Cook the gnocchi in the water for approximately 3 to 4 minutes; they will float when done. Remove the cooked gnocchi and let dry lightly on a towel.

To a large skillet, add a dollop of butter (1 tbsp or 14 g) and heat the skillet until the butter starts to sizzle. Gently sauté the gnocchi until lightly crisped.

Plate the dish with the Hazelnut Oil Pudding, Purple Potato Gnocchi, paper-thin shaved House-Cured Ham, Parmesan Sauce, and your favorite fresh herbs and fresh cracked black pepper.

ACORN CROQUETTES WITH BAKED CASHEWS

Possibly the dish that gets the most acclaim in our restaurant, smoked acorn croquettes are actually very easy to make and are a great food with drinks. I love noshing on the croquettes by themselves with a tepid smoked beer.

ACORN CROQUETTES
225 g (2 cups) acorns, shelled
2 tbsp marash pepper flakes*
1 tsp salt
190 ml (¾ cup) water
65 g (½ cups) flour
2 eggs, whisked
40 g (½ cups) panko bread
  crumbs

BAKED CASHEWS
6 tbsp butter
160 g (1 cup) onion, small dice
125 g (½ cup) bacon, chopped
1 garlic clove, minced
454 g (1 lb) cashews, whole
Rabbit Stock (p. 98)
125 ml (½ cup) maple syrup
125 ml (½ cup) malt vinegar
1 tsp dark mustard
1 inch fresh ginger, split in half
1 tbsp black pepper, freshly
  ground

ROASTED EGGPLANT
1 eggplant, peeled
neutral cooking oil, such as
  canola
2 tbsp salt, divided

MAKE ACORN CROQUETTES:

Place acorns in a food processor with the pepper flakes and salt. Begin grinding, and as the nuts begin to lump along the side of the processor bowl, drizzle the water onto the nuts. Add just enough water to make the nuts flow like a thick molten lava, leaving some rough texture. Let the mixture rest for 1 hour to allow absorption.

Form the nut paste into balls just a bit smaller than a ping-pong ball. Roll in the flour, then in egg wash, and finally in the panko. Rest in the refrigerator until ready to use, up to a day.

*NOTE: Marash is a moist pepper flake from Turkey. You can replace it with Aleppo or, in a pinch, ground dried New Mexico reds.

MAKE BAKED CASHEWS:

Preheat the oven to 325°F.

Sweat the onions in butter in a small stockpot over a medium heat until translucent. Add the bacon and stir for 5 minutes, being sure not to let the onions burn. Add the garlic and stir for 1 minute, then add the cashews and enough Rabbit Stock to cover the nuts plus a half an inch. Bring to a simmer and add the remaining ingredients. Return to a simmer and cook for 30 minutes or until the liquid has reduced to the level of the nuts. Place in the oven for 30 minutes uncovered.

MAKE ROASTED EGGLANT:

Preheat the oven to 325°F.

Cut eggplant into ½-inch slices crosswise, then quarter the slices. Layer the eggplant, with a heavy squirt of oil, in a loaf pan. Sprinkle with a pinch of salt, cover with foil, and bake in the oven for 45 minutes. Remove the roasted eggplant and put in the food processor. Process into a purée, adding salt to taste. If the eggplant is too dry, add additional oil to create a thick but flowing paste.

STEWED CHERRIES

150 g (1 cup) pitted cherries, fresh or frozen
250 ml (1 cup) water
3 green cardamom pods
1 tsp salt
1 tsp sugar
local goat cheese

Neutral oil, for frying slivered dried cherrywood

MAKE STEWED CHERRIES:

Combine all ingredients (except the goat cheese) in a small saucepan and bring to a simmer. Cook uncovered for 15 minutes or until liquid has evaporated.

To serve, heat a pot with 3 inches of frying oil to 350ºF. In a clamping Mason jar, place a dollop of the Roasted Eggplant on the bottom in the center. Around the Roasted Eggplant, add the Baked Cashews, followed by a couple of the Stewed Cherries and a small chunk of the goat cheese. Fry the Acorn Croquettes until golden brown and place on the Roasted Eggplant. Top with microgreens and Puffed Amaranth (p. 166). Use a smoking gun or Super-Aladín smoker to blow cherrywood smoke into the jar. Clamp the lid and serve. If you don't have the ability to blow smoke into the jar, you can create smoke in a metal loaf pan and capture in an upturned glass, which is then placed on top of the food on the plate.

SUGGESTED SUBSTITUTIONS: You can substitute most nuts in this recipe. We like the flavor of pecans when we run out of acorns.

100-LAYER SUMAC APPLES

In my early days, I fastidiously studied every book by Pierre Hermé, the famous French pastry chef. His work inspired me and taught me so many techniques that guide who I am today. Probably the best cookbook teacher ever—Dorie Greenspan—authored his English books, so I was in good hands. This recipe was inspired by his twenty-four-hour apple dessert, but I added a little foraged touch to bring it back to the savory side.

LAYERED APPLES
4 Granny Smith apples, peeled and whole
1 tbsp sumac powder
2-inch twig of pine tree

ONION GRANOLA
160 g (1 cup) onion, chopped
2 tbsp butter
64 g (½ cup) chickpea flour
½ tsp salt
1 egg white, room temperature

SWEET ONION SAUCE
160 g (1 cup) onion, chopped
2 tbsp butter
250 ml (1 cup) cream
salt, to taste

BROWN BUTTER POWDER
113 g (¼ cup) butter
20 g (1 cup) tapioca maltodextrin
salt, to taste

MAKE LAYERED APPLES:

Preheat the oven to 200°F.

Using a Chiba turning slicer (or a hand peeler), shave the apples into long ribbons. Line a loaf pan with aluminum foil. Carefully lay the apple ribbons onto the bottom of the pan, slightly overlapping each piece. Use your fingertips to cut the ribbons to the size and shape of the pan. About midway through the stack, sprinkle the apples with half of the sumac, then continue layering. Top the apples with the remaining sumac. Lay the pine twig on the top.

Wrap the pan in plastic wrap making sure that it has two layers and is airtight. I like to use one long piece instead of multiple pieces. Finally, wrap the pan in aluminum foil, ensuring that the pan is completely covered and no plastic wrap is exposed. This wrapping allows the apples to gently steam themselves without oxidizing. Bake for 6 hours. Remove the pine twig and then rest until just slightly warmer than room temperature.

MAKE ONION GRANOLA:

Preheat the oven to 300°F.

In a medium saucepan, sauté the onion in the butter, stirring regularly, until the onions are medium brown. Remove from heat and let cool slightly. Add the chickpea flour and salt and stir until a thick paste is formed. Add the egg white, which will loosen the paste some, but it will still remain thick. Spread the paste over a baking sheet. Bake 15 minutes, then using a fork, break up the paste into granola-sized pieces. Return the pan for an additional 15 minutes or until the granola browns. Let cool to room temperature.

MAKE SWEET ONION SAUCE:

In a medium saucepan, sauté the onion in the butter, stirring regularly, until the onions are dark brown. Add the cream and bring to a simmer. Let cook on medium-low until it reduced by about half and thickens slightly. Salt to taste. Put the mixture in a blender and process until smooth. Hold until ready to use.

MAKE BROWN BUTTER POWDER:

Cook the butter in a medium saucepan until dark brown. Don't skimp on the browning process, because the flavor is going to come from the darkness. Let the butter cool to room temperature, keeping it from resolidifying.

In a large mixing bowl, add the tapioca maltodextrin, being careful to not have it fly up and be inhaled. While slowly whisking, drizzle a little bit of the browned butter into the powder. Stop drizzling and whisk thoroughly to make sure that no butter is pooled at the bottom. Continue drizzling while whisking, until the powder begins to clump and look like snow. You may not use all of the butter. Let the final texture be your guide. You want light lumps, not floating powder. Add the salt and whisk again. Store the powder in an airtight container until ready to use.

To serve, spread a spoonful of the Sweet Onion Sauce on the plate. Cut a 1-inch square of the Layered Apples and place it on top of the sauce. Sprinkle the Onion Granola and Brown Butter Powder on top. Finally, we like to add fresh clover microgreens, and you can, too.

MESQUITE CHOCOLATE CHIP COOKIES

A few years ago, a customer was on hospice with cancer and was not able to leave her home because of her frail health. Her husband was regularly making runs to get meals and snacks from me to comfort his wife in her final days. One afternoon, while he napped, she sneaked into the kitchen, grabbed the car keys, and very slowly drove the two miles to our restaurant, where she bought a dozen of these cookies. When her husband woke up, six cookies had been eaten and crumbs left on her bed covers. Her husband asked who had visited while he was asleep. "No one. I had to have one more cookie," she sheepishly explained, knowing she did something she shouldn't have. Her husband scolded her, but then helped her enjoy the last six.

These cookies are special because of the mesquite, but are also great because of the combination of the muscovado, the browned butter, and the overnight hydration.

   12

454 g (2 cups) unsalted butter
454 g (2 cups) muscovado sugar
180 g (¾ cup) white sugar
2 eggs
2 egg yolks
125 ml (½ cup) milk
2 tbsp vanilla extract
480 g (3¾ cups) all-purpose
 flour
75 g (¾ cup) mesquite flour
 (p. 35)
80 g (¾ cup) oat flour (grind
 oats in food processor)
1 tbsp salt
2 tsp baking powder
1 tsp baking soda
342 g (2¼ cups) dark chocolate
 chips

Brown the butter in a saucepan. The browner, the better! I like to gently run a whisk through the pan, starting when the butter is all melted, to make sure that it doesn't burn on the bottom, but then letting it get chestnut brown or maybe a bit darker. Color is flavor! Once you have your desired darkness, pour the butter over the sugars in a large mixing bowl. Carefully stir, making sure you don't splash hot butter on yourself, and stir until blended. Let the slurry rest until it is no longer hot and won't melt the chocolate chips when added, about 30 minutes.

In a separate mixing bowl, combine the eggs, yolks, milk, and vanilla. Whisk to combine. Pour into butter mixture and stir until homogenous.

Combine the remaining dry ingredients in a separate bowl. Pour the dry ingredients over the wet mixture and stir gently until almost but not quite combined. One of the keys to making great pastries is not overmixing, and this is one of those instances.

We buy a variety of chocolate chips, but prefer those in the 70 percent range. If you don't have specific options, you can just buy the darkest chocolate bar you can find (such as a Lindt 85 percent bar) and chop it into small chunks. Add the chocolate to the mixture and finish stirring until thoroughly combined. Using an ice cream scoop, portion the dough onto a parchment-lined pan and chill in your refrigerator overnight. This overnight process ages, or hydrates, the dough, allowing for much deeper flavor. The chilling process also allows your cookies to keep their shape while baking. When you're ready to bake, preheat the oven to 350°F, and bake on a lined sheet pan for 25 to 30 minutes or until brown.

SUGGESTED SUBSTITUTIONS: Muscovado can be replaced by an equal amount of brown sugar with 1 tablespoon molasses. Mesquite flour is readily available online; however, you can also substitute an equal amount of oat flour in addition to the original oat flour in the recipe.

MESQUITE SUMAC SHORTBREAD

A simple little cookie, but the flavors are a perfect combination. A young mesquite has a strong citrus flavor, and by combining it with the sour sumac, you create a sort of sweet and sour lemonade cookie. When I want to freak out my burly beer drinkers, I give them a fresh cookie sprinkled with salt and a good sour Belgian ale. Now that's my type of bar food!

90 g (¾ cup) powdered sugar
2 tbsp sumac powder
84 g (½ cup + 2 tbsp) butter, softened and cut into ¼-inch cubes
2 egg yolks, room temperature
160 g (1¼ cups) all-purpose flour
63 g (½ cup) mesquite flour (p. 35)

Using a stand mixer fitted with the paddle attachment, combine the sugar and sumac. Add the butter and mix until combined, working quickly so as not to warm the butter any more than necessary. Add the yolks and mix until well blended. Add both flours and mix until just combined, but no more. Shortbreads become tough when overmixed.

Very lightly sprinkle additional flour on a Silpat and roll the dough to ½-inch thickness by first placing parchment paper on top to prevent the dough from sticking to the rolling pin. Cut the dough into your desired shapes and freeze for 10 minutes.

Preheat the oven to 350°F.

Bake for 15 minutes or until just lightly browned on the bottom. For a cookie sandwich, fill with the Sweet Corn Sumac Cayenne Ganache (p. 128).

ACORN FINANCIERS

I serve these at the beginning of a meal, even though they are sweet. Acorn has a back-of-your-tongue bitterness that will start your meal off right. All the senses are activated with this tiny little treat: sweet, rich, warm, crisp, gooey, moist. All first bites should be this good.

168 g (¾ cup) butter
220 g (1 cup) sugar
125 g (1 cup) acorn flour (p. 31)
128 g (1 cup) cake flour
2 tsp baking powder
salt, to taste
7 egg whites

Brown the butter in a saucepan and let cool to room temperature. In a mixing bowl, whisk the sugar, acorn flour, cake flour, baking powder, and a pinch of salt. Add the butter and egg whites to the dry ingredients, and using a stand mixer fitted with the paddle attachment, mix on low until combined. Increase the speed to medium-high and whip until lightened in color. Transfer the batter to a pastry bag or zip top bag and chill for at least 1 hour.

Preheat the oven to 425°F.

Pipe the batter into a buttered muffin tin or silicone mold and bake for 8 minutes. Reduce the heat to 375°F and bake an additional 8 minutes or until firm but springy to the touch.

SUGGESTED SUBSTITUTIONS: Instead of acorn flour, you can also use mesquite, almond, or hazelnut meal in equal amounts.

ACORN CHOCOLATE PUDDING

Know your culinary esoterica! From these fringe corners, you find great inspiration. I was looking for international uses of acorns and came across the Korean dotorimuk—acorn jelly. Then, around the same time, I needed to make a vegan chocolate dessert for a customer. The two ideas led me to a vegan chocolate pudding. In this version, I've used nonvegan chocolate, but simply using 100 percent chocolate (cocoa mass) with ¼ cup sugar will please your vegan friends.

750 ml (3 cups) water
63 g (½ cup) acorn starch* (p. 31)
75 g (½ cup) 65% chocolate chips
2 tbsp honey
pinch of salt

Bring the water to a simmer. Sift in the acorn flour, whisking constantly. The mixture will become a thick porridge very quickly, so whisk diligently. Continue cooking for 5 minutes while the acorn mixture sputters and splatters.

To a medium mixing bowl, add the chocolate and honey, and salt. Pour the hot acorn slurry over the chocolate and let rest for 1 minute. Gently but thoroughly stir until homogenous. If lumps form, pass the pudding through a sieve to end up with a smooth mixture. Serve warm with toasted pine nuts and a shot of *nocino* if you have them. You can also let this cool to room temperature and then fold into 2 cups of whipped cream to make a mousse.

*NOTE: If using your own acorn starch, be sure that it is the finest grind possible. For most recipes, I use acorn in a cornmeal texture, but that's not fine enough for this recipe. Grind as fine as you can then run through a sieve. This recipe is ideal for using acorn starch purchased from an Asian grocery.

SUGGESTED SUBSTITUTIONS: This recipe was designed for acorn starch and doesn't work with other starches such as potato or corn. So if you can't find acorn starch, skip the recipe.

HACKBERRY POT DE CRÈME

Hackberries have a strong similarity to dates. They're flavor-packed, sweet, and plentiful, making them a great foraged item. The downside is that there is virtually no meat on the bones, so use them as a steeping flavor.

HACKBERRY POT DE CRÈME
375 ml (1½ cups) cream
135 g (1 cup) hackberries, dried (p. 34)
55 g (¼ cup) sugar
6 egg yolks
1 tbsp vanilla

PUFFED AMARANTH
150 g (2 cups) amaranth seeds or purchased puffed amaranth (p. 203)
224 g (1 cup) butter
400 g (2 cups) brown sugar, packed
1 tsp salt
125 ml (½ cup) corn syrup
1 tsp baking soda

MAKE HACKBERRY POT DE CRÈME:

Bring cream to a simmer in a medium saucepan. Add hackberries, remove from heat, and cover. Allow to steep for 1 hour. Strain the berries and hold the cream at a simmer.

In a medium-sized mixing bowl, combine the sugar and yolks, whisking until lightly foamy.

Pour a third of the hot cream into the yolk and sugar mixture, whisking constantly. Pour the hot yolk and sugar mixture back into the remaining hot cream. Whisk gently. Continue cooking over medium heat until the mixture thickens slightly. You want thickened, but not curdled.

Pour the pudding through a fine mesh strainer to remove any lumps. Add the vanilla and whisk to disperse, and then pour into your serving dish, covering with plastic wrap to prevent a skin from forming. Allow the pudding to cool to room temperature. Transfer to your refrigerator to chill.

> **SUGGESTED SUBSTITUTIONS:** If you can't get hackberries, buy dried dates and replace by volume.

MAKE PUFFED AMARANTH:

If you are puffing your own seeds, soak them in water and let rest overnight. Spread thinly on a kitchen counter and let air-dry during the day. Soak them a second time overnight. Again, air-dry, but this time only for a few hours, tousling them to make sure that all seeds are dry to the touch. What this process attempts to do is soften the cell structure and expand the puffing capacity. Think of the process as what you do to stretch a balloon prior to inflating it.

Heat a large cast-iron skillet over very high heat. Dampen a paper towel with cooking oil and wipe the inside of the pan. You want a coating of oil but no standing oil. Working with ¼ cup of seeds at a time, pour the seeds into the pan, stirring with a spoon until they puff like miniature popcorn. Continue until all amaranth is popped, and place amaranth in a large mixing bowl. The fresher the seeds, the larger they will pop.

Preheat the oven to 200°F.

In a medium saucepan, combine the butter, sugar, salt, and corn syrup. Bring to a boil and continue boiling for 5 minutes. Remove the pan from the heat and add the baking soda. Stir quickly but thoroughly. Pour the caramel over the puffed amaranth, and quickly but gently stir to coat.

Spread caramelized amaranth onto a baking sheet and place in the oven. Bake for 1 hour, stirring every 15 minutes. After 1 hour, pour the amaranth on a sheet of parchment paper to cool.

Mound a handful of caramel amaranth on top of the pot de crème and enjoy.

NOTE: Amaranth is a superfood worth exploring. In the spring, you get tender delicious greens, and in the winter, nutritious seeds. The seeds are much smaller than sesame seeds and the winnowing process is a heart-breaking experience. Buying amaranth seed from your local market or online is prudent.

BUTTERSCOTCH PIE WITH CANDIED BLACK WALNUTS

The problem with most butterscotch recipes is that they use artificial flavors either by melting butterscotch candy or adding extracts. I wanted a pure, natural flavor that convinces the mind into thinking it is butterscotch. Enjoy this in a pie shell, warm in a cup, or as a filling between two cake layers. And a nod to Chef Jonah Rhodehamel at Oliveto in Oakland who served me an amazing butterscotch with crumbled toffee bits and brown butter espuma—swoon!

BUTTERSCOTCH PIE
500 ml (2 cups) heavy cream
110 g (½ cup) muscovado sugar
9 egg yolks
2 tbsp butter, room temperature
65 ml (¼ cup) whiskey*

CANDIED BLACK WALNUTS
120 g (1 cup) black walnuts,
    shelled (p. 37)
500 ml (2 cups) water
220 g (1 cup) sugar

MAKE BUTTERSCOTCH PIE:

Bring the cream to a simmer in a saucepan and hold warm. On the bottom of a larger saucepan, spread the muscovado sugar. Heat the pan on medium-low and watch the sugar extremely closely. The sugar will go from dry to burnt in seconds, so nudge it around with a whisk while you're waiting for it to melt. If you have a hot spot in your pan, move the sugar to and from it. The very moment the sugar is pretty much melted, pour a third of the cream into the sugar to stop it from burning. Be careful as it splashes and sputters. Whisk gently until homogenous. Add the remaining cream and whisk until the eruption calms down and sputters gently.

While you're waiting for the pot to calm down, place the yolks in a mixing bowl. Temper the yolks by pouring a third of the hot cream mixture into the yolks and whisk until combined. Pour the hot yolk mixture into the rest of the hot cream and then return to the stove. Whisk constantly until the pudding begins to thicken. It's important to remove the pudding as it just starts to thicken; otherwise, you can curdle your dessert. Pour the pudding through a strainer into a mixing bowl. Add the butter and whiskey and whisk until incorporated. Pour into a serving dish. If using as a cake filling, add three sheets of softened silver gelatin to set.

MAKE CANDIED BLACK WALNUTS:

Preheat the oven to 275°F.

Place all of the items in a saucepan and bring to a simmer. Continue simmering for 10 minutes. Strain the nuts, keeping the syrup for your coffee. Lay the nuts on a baking sheet and bake for 30 minutes or until fragrant, shaking the pan every 10 minutes. Remove from the oven and let cool.

Sprinkle the nuts on top of the butterscotch and enjoy.

*NOTE: Use locally distilled whiskey. We love Don Quixote blue corn bourbon from Los Alamos, New Mexico.

SPRUCE CHOCOLATE RAVIOLI

Spruce tips are all the rage in the culinary world, but heaven forbid you do the obvious pairing with citrus that screams floor cleaner. But there is a reason why spruce has emerged—it tastes good and has a fantastic texture. This recipe taps into the flavor and sends it in a different direction by pairing the spruce with a dark rich chocolate, reminding me of some amazing Italian mountain cakes. Use the remaining oil in other dishes, especially with fish and seafood.

BLOOD ORANGE SAUCE
250 ml (1 cup) blood orange juice, divided
1 tbsp cornstarch
1 tbsp unsalted butter
pinch of salt

SPRUCE OIL
250 ml (1 cup) neutral cooking oil, such as canola
50 g (1 cup) spruce tips (p. 36)

SPRUCE GANACHE
170 ml (⅔ cup) cream
262 g (1¾ cups) white chocolate chips
2 tbsp Spruce Oil

CHOCOLATE PASTA
128 g (1 cup) whole wheat flour
64 g (½ cup) semolina flour
64 g (½ cup) black cocoa powder
30 g (¼ cup) powdered sugar
1 tsp salt, plus more as needed
3 eggs
220 g (1 cup) sugar
1 egg, beaten for egg wash
black pepper, to taste

MAKE BLOOD ORANGE SAUCE:

Place ¼ cup of the blood orange juice in a small bowl and whisk in the cornstarch to make a slurry. Heat the remaining juice in a small saucepan. Add the slurry to the saucepan and simmer, whisking constantly, until slightly thickened. Remove from the heat and add the butter and salt. Hold until ready to serve.

MAKE SPRUCE OIL:

Place the oil and spruce tips in a small saucepan and heat to just warm to the touch. Remove from the heat and cover. Let steep 2 hours. Remove the tips (which can be enjoyed in an omelet or in a salad) and run the oil through a paper coffee filter to remove any lasting debris. Hold refrigerated up to 1 week.

MAKE SPRUCE GANACHE:

Bring cream to a simmer in a small saucepan. Place white chocolate into a food processor and grind into coarse pieces. Pour the hot cream over the chocolate and let rest for 30 seconds. Process until smooth, and while the food processor is running, drizzle in the spruce oil. Transfer to a piping bag and let rest until slightly firm, squeezing the bag from time to time to redistribute the warm ganache from the thinnest to the thickest part of the bag.

MAKE CHOCOLATE PASTA:

Whisk together the flours, cocoa, sugar, and salt in a mixing bowl. Pour onto a kitchen counter and make a well in the center of the dry ingredients. Crack the eggs into the well and gently whisk with a fork. As you whisk, slowly begin pulling in some of the dry ingredients to combine with the egg. Increasingly bring in more dry ingredients until you can no longer whisk with a fork, and then switch to your fingers. I like to have one messy hand and one hand holding a pastry scraper to clean my fingers as I go. Continue until you have a homogenous mass of dough that can be kneaded. The dough will be gritty and dry at first, but keep working on it and it will smooth out but remain firm. Knead for 5 minutes or until smooth. Add more flour or a bit of water as needed to get an elastic, but not sticky, consistency. Wrap securely in plastic wrap and store for 1 hour at room temperature.

Cut off a lump of dough about the size of a golf ball, flatten it with your hand, and then roll it through a pasta roller or with a rolling pin to ¹⁄₁₆-inch thick, creating a long strip of pasta. Pipe 1 tablespoon of the firmed Spruce Ganache into mounds 2 inches apart from one another on the strip, and brush around the ganache with egg wash. Roll a second strip of pasta and lay it on top of the ganache. Use a ravioli cutter to seal and cut your ravioli. Let the ravioli sit on a drying rack on the counter to form a skin on the pasta and allow the egg wash to seal the top and bottom. Conversely, you can cut your pasta into linguine and form the ganache into "meatballs" to serve.

Fill a stockpot with 1 gallon of water and add the sugar. Bring to a boil. Add the ravioli and cook 8 to 10 minutes or until al dente.

To serve, plate the pasta with the blood orange sauce and drizzle with the Spruce Oil. Sprinkle with salt and pepper.

SUGGESTED SUBSTITUTIONS: If you don't have access to spruce, you can try other evergreens, but always harvest the new spring tips when the flavor is delicate.

YUCCA BLOSSOM ICE CREAM WITH MESQUITE COUSCOUS

I was raised in a family that would down a half-gallon of ice cream every night. We leaned butter pecan or rocky road but really, any ice cream did the trick. But for me, I always wanted texture with my ice cream. I watch people sensually licking their cones as their tongue swoops its imprint over the soft cream and think, "Wouldn't that be better with some nuts or sprinkles?" I reach for the subtle sweetness of mesquite to do the trick with my Yucca Blossom Ice Cream.

MESQUITE COUSCOUS

- 448 g (3½ cups) all-purpose flour
- 63 g (½ cup) mesquite flour (p. 35)
- 4 large eggs
- 2 egg whites

YUCCA BLOSSOM ICE CREAM

- 250 ml (1 cup) milk
- 160 g (1 cup) yucca blossoms, chopped (p. 37)
- 250 ml (1 cup) cream
- 190 ml (¾ cup) buckwheat honey
- 6 egg yolks
- 1 tsp salt
- 220 g (1 cup) sugar

MAKE MESQUITE COUSCOUS:

Whisk the flours together and pour into a mound on your countertop. Make a well in the center. In a bowl, lightly whisk the eggs and egg whites. Pour the eggs into the center of the flours. Using a fork, mix the eggs with the flours, gradually working your way from the center to the outside. When the mixture becomes too cumbersome with your fork, switch to using your fingers. Once combined, knead the couscous dough for 5 minutes and wrap in plastic wrap. Let rest 30 minutes.

Roll the dough to ⅛-inch thickness and chop with a knife as if you were mincing herbs, keeping the pasta about the size of a BB-gun pellet. Let the chopped couscous rest uncovered to dry slightly.

MAKE YUCCA BLOSSOM ICE CREAM:

Place the milk and blossoms in a saucepan and bring to a simmer. Cover and remove from the heat, steeping for 1 hour. Strain the blossoms out of the milk and combine the milk, cream, and honey, bringing to a simmer again. In a bowl, combine the yolks and salt and whisk until light and frothy. Pour a third of the hot milk mixture into the yolks, whisking constantly, and return the hot yolks to the remaining milk mixture. Continue whisking gently until the ice cream base is slightly thickened. Remove from the heat, cover, and let cool in the refrigerator overnight.

The next day, freeze the ice cream in an ice-cream maker and transfer the ice cream to a container to freeze until firm.

To serve, fill a small stockpot with water and add 220 g (1 cup) sugar. Bring to a boil. Add the couscous, being sure to break up the pieces before they go into the water. Boil for 5 minutes. Serve the ice cream drizzled with Pine Cone Syrup (p. 191) over the couscous after a meal of spicy goat tagine.

LEMON POPPY SEED BONBONS

These little chocolates take all that is good with the classic lemon poppy seed muffin and turn it into a dainty little treat. Enjoy these with hot tea on a cloudy afternoon.

See chocolate tempering instructions on p. 85.
125 ml (½ cup) meyer lemon juice
65 ml (¼ cup) corn syrup
225 g (1½ cups) white chocolate (we use El Rey), chopped
1 tbsp unsalted butter, room temperature
1 tbsp poppy seeds, toasted (p. 204)

Bring the juice and syrup to a simmer for 2 minutes. Remove from heat and let rest for 1 minute. Place chocolate in a food processor and grind to small pebbles. Slowly pour the hot juice mixture over the chocolate and process until smooth. Add the butter and process until no butter shows. Add the poppy seeds, stirring to incorporate, and transfer to a piping bag. Pipe into prepared chocolate molds and let set overnight. Spread a thin layer of tempered chocolate onto the bottom of the molds to cap the bonbons; allow to set firm and serve.

CASSIS POPPY SEED BONBONS

While Americans love their desserts sweet, Europeans prefer more subtlety in their treats. Cassis (black currant) is one of the beneficiaries of that palate, because it offers some sweetness but is more about an earthy tartness. I like using cassis with white chocolate for the balance as well as the beautiful color they create together.

POPPY SEED GANACHE

See chocolate tempering instructions on p. 85.
240 g (1½ cups) poppy seeds, toasted (p. 204)
165 g (¾ cup) sugar
125 ml (½ cup) milk
½ tsp salt
150 g (1 cup) white chocolate, chopped
56 g (¼ cup) butter, room temperature

CASSIS CHOCOLATE

125 ml (½ cup) cream
65 ml (¼ cup) cassis (black currant) purée
2 tbsp corn syrup
99 g (⅔ cup) 65% chocolate, chopped
37 g (¼ cup) milk chocolate, chopped
1 tsp cherry liqueur
42 g (3 tbsp) unsalted butter, softened

Grind the poppy seeds in the bowl of a blade coffee grinder. In a small saucepan, combine ground poppy seeds, sugar, milk, and salt. Bring to a simmer. Place in a blender and process for 2 minutes. Add the white chocolate and process until smooth. Add the butter and process once again. Transfer to a pastry bag and let cool until at room temperature. Pipe into prepared chocolate molds, filling just halfway up the shell. Let set up overnight.

Bring cream, cassis purée, and corn syrup to a simmer. Let rest 1 minute. Place chocolates in the bowl of a food processor and grind into small pebbles. Pour cassis cream over the ground chocolates and process until smooth. Add the liqueur and the unsalted butter and process again. Transfer to a pastry bag and cool to room temperature. Pipe on top of the prepared poppy seed ganache, and let the new layer set up overnight. Spread a thin layer of tempered chocolate onto the bottom of the molds to cap the bonbons; allow to set firm and serve.

HACKBERRY SODA

Here's a fast, easy soda that's perfect for watching the sun set during an Indian summer night. It's refreshing and comforting, with a deep, rich flavor and light citrus accent.

270 g (2 cups) hackberries
   (p. 34)
250 ml (1 cup) water
73 g (⅓ cup) muscovado sugar
soda water
lemon peel

Place hackberries, water, and sugar in a large saucepan and simmer for 30 minutes, or until reduced by half. Strain solids out and use remaining liquid as a base concentrate for the soda. To make the final soda, fill a glass halfway with the base concentrate and finish with soda water and a strip of lemon peel. Stir.

SUGGESTED SUBSTITUTIONS: Hackberries can be replaced with dried dates.

ROOT BEER FLOAT

This recipe is packed with foraged plants and maximizes the flora that is so plentiful across much of the country. While not really ice cream nor a float, this combination of mousses and creams creates a modern dessert while tipping its cap to a classic treat. You can use the root-beer base for a fresh soda by thinning it with soda water or even a sparkling white wine. This recipe takes time, but is worth it.

ROOT-BEER BASE
34 g (¼ cup) sassafras root
2 tbsp dandelion root
1 tbsp wintergreen leaf
2 tbsp hops
34 g (¼ cup) juniper berries
220 g (1 cup) sugar
220 g (1 cup) muscovado sugar
220 g (1 cup) palm sugar
160 g (½ cup) buckwheat honey

ICE CREAM
190 ml (¾ cup) whole milk
55 g (¼ cup) sugar
2 egg yolks
1 tbsp vanilla paste
5 sheets silver gelatin (5 tsp powder), softened
190 ml (¾ cup) cream

ROOT-BEER CREAM
190 ml (¾ cup) cream
2 tbsp root beer base
3 egg yolks
1 sheet silver gelatin (1 tsp powder), softened

MAKE ROOT-BEER BASE:

Rinse the sassafras and dandelion roots under cold water. Crush the juniper berries to release the oils. Wrap all of the herbs and berries (sassafras through juniper) in a cheesecloth bag. Bring 2 gallons of water to a boil. In a separate pot, pour 1 gallon of the boiled water over the seasoning bag and bring to a simmer. Simmer for 30 minutes.

Remove the bag and discard. Add the sugars, honey, and the remaining gallon of water. Taste the base and make adjustments for sweetness and acidity. As you continue cooking, the liquid will concentrate, which will make the flavors more pronounced. So if a flavor is weak at this stage, add more of it to increase its prevalence in the final product. Return the pot to a simmer and cook down until slightly thickened, around 2 hours. Cool to room temperature. This base can now be used for a variety of recipes, including as a breakfast syrup.

MAKE ICE CREAM:

Bring milk to a simmer and hold. In a mixing bowl, combine the sugar and yolks. Pour a third of the hot milk into the yolk mixture and whisk. Return the tempered yolks to the remaining milk and whisk constantly over medium heat until slightly thickened. Don't let the sauce curdle. Remove the milk mixture from heat and add the vanilla paste and gelatin. Whisk gently to combine. Cover with film and allow this sauce to cool to room temperature. Whip the cream to soft peaks. Place a quarter of the whipped cream in the milk mixture and fold to combine. Then put all of the milk mixture that has been tempered with the cream into the remaining cream and fold carefully. Pour into your favorite shaped silicon mold or lined muffin tin.

MAKE ROOT-BEER CREAM:

Bring the cream to a simmer and hold. In a separate bowl, combine the syrup and yolks. Temper the yolks as described in the ice-cream instructions where you prepare the yolks for the hot liquid by adding a third of the hot cream first before returning the tempered yolks to the remaining cream. Whisk in the gelatin and cool until it begins to thicken. Pour into your favorite shaped silicon mold or lined muffin tin.

CHERRY

250 ml (1 cup) maraschino
cherry juice

1½ tsp calcium lactate

2 tbsp sugar

1 liter (4½ cups) water

2 tsp sodium alginate

MAKE THE CHERRY:

Place the juice and calcium lactate in a large measuring cup and stir until dissolved. Pipe the juice into a 1-inch sphere mold and freeze until solid.

In a blender, combine the sugar, water, and sodium alginate, scraping the sides to ensure that all of the alginate is blended. Let rest 30 minutes to disperse the air bubbles. Drop the frozen cherry balls in the sodium alginate bath for 45 seconds. Carefully remove the spheres, being careful not to puncture the slimy skin, and place in a dish filled with plain water. The cherry balls will thaw in about 30 minutes. Hold the liquid-filled balls, chilled, until ready to serve.

Remove the root-beer cream and ice cream from the freezer a few hours before serving, allowing to thaw. Plate with the cherry spheres, a maraschino cherry, and toasted nuts.

SUGGESTED SUBSTITUTIONS: There are root-beer bases that you can buy online, as well as extracts.

NOCINO

Make this recipe ever year, and each year you can blend your new and old batches to create a stunning after-dinner drink. The process is also fun to watch as your jar goes from clear to pitch black in days.

   10

30 green walnuts (p. 37)
2 cinnamon sticks
5 cloves, whole
peel of 1 lemon
800 g (2½ cups) muscovado
    sugar
1 liter (4½ cups) 100-proof
    vodka

Carefully cut the walnuts in half with a sturdy knife. Toast the cinnamon and cloves in a skillet until fragrant. Place the cut walnuts, toasted spices, and all remaining ingredients in a large Mason jar with a lid. Store for a month, shaking daily. After just a few days, the vodka will discolor into a dark brown.

After a month, strain out the solids and sneak a quick taste. The flavor should be harsh at this point; adjust the sweetness, realizing that the flavor will mellow over time. Replace the tight-fitting lid with gauze strapped with a rubber band to allow for evaporation. Our tradition is to taste the *nocino* on Christmas Eve. Since I make *nocino* every year, I like to blend my various years to make the perfect combination of sweetness, citrus, and astringency. Enjoy with aged, hard cheese in front of a fire.

GINNED TOMATOES

You planted those cherry tomatoes, and now you can't eat them as fast as they're growing. This snack takes a bit of effort to peel all the tomatoes but is well worth it, as the bite-sized juice explosions will delight your friends.

CONCENTRATE

12 inches popotillo branch (Mormon tea)
34 g (¼ cup) juniper berries
2 tbsp pine needles
2 tbsp fresh mint
20 g (¼ cup) cilantro
zest of 1 lime
1 green chile, roasted, whole (heat level to your taste)
1 L (4½ cups) 100-proof vodka

GINNED TOMATOES

454 g (1 lb) cherry tomatoes
500 ml (2 cups) gin
1 tsp salt

MAKE CONCENTRATE:

With a mortar and pestle, bruise and pound all the ingredients except the vodka to release their oils and juices. Place the ingredients in a jar large enough that the plants can be submerged.

Pour half the vodka over bruised ingredients, cover loosely, and let steep for 4 days. During those 4 days, shake or stir the mixture a few times each day. On the last day, strain the mixture through a coffee filter or run through your water filter. This is the concentrate.

Finally, add the remaining vodka to the concentrate, and you're ready to go.

MAKE GINNED TOMATOES:

Bring a pan of water to a simmer. Fill a bowl with ice water. Score each cherry tomato on its bottom (opposite of the stem side) with a small X, just cutting through the skin. Drop the tomatoes into the hot, simmering water and cook for 30 seconds. Remove the tomatoes quickly and dunk in the ice water. Peel the skin off the tomatoes and place tomatoes in a clean bowl. Dissolve the salt in the gin. Pour the salted gin over the tomatoes and let rest at room temperature overnight.

Enjoy these as finger food with cubed cheese or in a martini.

SUGGESTED SUBSTITUTIONS: Make the gin your own using whatever is around. Mormon tea is the only ingredient that might be challenging to find, so try birch branches or even local hay.

FORAGED LIQUEUR

Many amazing flavors in the wilderness lend themselves to great drinks. Use this list as a jumping-off point for items in your neck of the woods. The gin concentrate recipe (p. 184) can be used as a base recipe, adjusting proportions to your personal tastes.

ACORN: Dark rum, Okinawa black sugar, tangerine

MINT: Light rum, white sugar, pineapple

HOREHOUND: Vodka, brown sugar, black peppercorns

PRICKLY PEAR: Tequila, agave syrup

CHOLLA FRUIT: Vodka, sage

GRAPE MUST: Ouzo, lemon

With any of these suggested combinations, tease the flavor out of the ingredients by toasting or bruising. Add the ingredients to the liquor and steep from 1 month to up to a year. Let your judgment and tongue guide your choices.

5 | GARNISH
AND FLAIR
RECIPES

As a result of our restaurant's remote location, I grow, forage, pick, gather, cut, process, cure, roast, plate, serve, clean, and do the dishes. On a daily basis, I make no fewer than seventy-five recipes. To maintain my sanity in the midst of this daunting schedule and to provide a bit of efficiency, I make a number of items ahead of time and store them for later use. Here are a number of basic recipes that you can use to "finish" your dishes and give them extra flair without overtaxing your cooking life.

ASHES

Cattail fronds make my favorite ash, but you can use wild garlic, leek, ramps, rose hips, or some tree barks, such as birch. Regardless of which you use, brush off any unwanted or damaged material and clean the plant well. Place on a dry baking sheet and set in a 475°F oven. Bake until the material just starts to turn dark brown or black. This will take anywhere from 15 minutes to nearly 1 hour, depending on what you're turning to ash. The goal is to remove the moisture but not burn the material. Once darkened, remove from the oven and let rest until it reaches room temperature.

Using either a mortar and pestle or stainless steel-blade coffee grinder, grind into a fine powder. This is your base ash. Store the ash in an airtight container for up to a year. For a dry condiment, combine three parts ash to one part fine sea salt. The dry ash salt can be sprinkled on any food, but is particularly nice on melon. For ash paint, combine two parts ash with one part neutral cooking oil and one part salt. Mix it into a slurry and store. The ash paint can be used as plating decoration or brushed on meats and vegetables. I like brushing potatoes with the ash while they're roasting.

FOUR-WING SALTBUSH

One of the journeys we took in our restaurant history was replacing bought salt with found salt. Since we're in the desert, sea salt wasn't an option, but a plentiful option exists in four-wing saltbush. The easiest treatment is to turn the leaves into an ash as outlined above and mix with a bit of oil to create a slurry. But we also like to brine our meats in a pot filled with saltbush branches. If you're feeling especially adventurous, soak a few layers of burlap in water, cover the burlap with ample saltbush branches, and place a butchered whole baby goat in the center. Tie up the meat in the burlap and roast in the ground overnight—the best cabrito you'll ever have!

PINE CONE SYRUP

Not all pine cones are created equal. Learn your local pine cones (we prefer Ponderosa pines), and experiment to find which time of year gives you the best flavor. Drop the pine cones in boiling water for 30 seconds. Remove and repeat in a fresh pot of water. This will remove some of the dirt, break up the sticky sap, and leave you with purer flavor. To make a simple syrup, use equal parts sugar and water. Bring sugar water to a boil in a large saucepan over medium heat. Once at a boil, add a handful of previously blanched pine cones, cover, and simmer for 30 minutes. Remove from the heat, cover, and let rest for 2 hours. Strain the syrup through a paper coffee filter. This may take as long as overnight. Store in an airtight container for up to a week.

SMOKED BUTTER

If you have access to quality butter then don't bother making your own, but most of us are stuck with regional mega-dairy butter that is mostly flavorless.

However, making butter is not difficult. At its core, simply whip cream until it transitions from light and fluffy to broken and messy. Making it special, however, takes a few extra steps.

Start by buying good-quality cream from your local farmer. Pour a quart of cream in a 9 × 13 or hotel pan. Cover the top tightly with plastic wrap. Check to make sure the wrap is secure enough to hold in the smoke, and if needed add extra layers of wrap. If you have a Smoking Gun or Super-Aladín smoker, burn cherry wood or mesquite chips and blow the smoke under the film through an opened corner. Reseal tightly. Let rest overnight in your fridge.

If you don't have a Smoking Gun or Super-Aladín smoker, roll back the wrap to expose the center of the pan. Fill the 9 × 13 pan with cream and place a small heatproof bowl in the center of the pan. Be sure that the bowl sits lower than the rim of the pan, so air can circulate when the plastic wrap is covering the top again. Place cherrywood or mesquite chips in the bowl and light the wood on fire, letting it burn until only smoldering flames remain. Douse the flame with water, being sure not to splatter ash into the cream. This will create the smoke. Very quickly and securely, pull the wrap back over the entire pan and make air-tight. With this method, it is best to do a second and even a third layer of wrap to lock the smoke in. Let rest overnight in your fridge.

Regardless of how you smoke the cream, place the smoked, chilled cream in the bowl of a mixer. Start whisking as though making whipped cream, starting on low and gradually increasing the speed. Once the

cream turns to soft peaks, begin watching the cream diligently. A few minutes more and the cream will stiffen. At this point, partially cover the top of the bowl by holding a kitchen towel draped above to prevent splashing. Continue whisking on medium-high speed. Eventually the cream will separate into liquid and solid—you've just made butter!

Strain the butter from the liquid, and transfer the solid butter to your kitchen counter. We like to use the remaining buttermilk in a ceviche with jalapeños, fresh currant, lime, and cattail ash salt.

Knead the butter on a flour sack towel for a bit to work out the remaining liquid, and then wrap the butter in a cheesecloth. I like to use the wedding veils sold at Wal-Mart because they are cheap, reusable, and easy to clean. Shape the wrapped butter into either a roll or block and store.

The final step for overachievers is to roll the butter in ash, dehydrated vegetable powders, or even kaolin clay powder.

SWEET CORN BUTTER

Cut the kernels from two ears of fresh sweet corn. Pour a quart of cream in a large saucepan with the corn cobs and kernels. Bring to a simmer, remove from the heat, and steep, covered, for 1 hour. Strain corn and cobs from the cream and chill the cream in your fridge for 3 hours.

Place the chilled cream in the bowl of a stand mixer fitted with the whisk attachment. Start whisking as though making whipped cream, starting on low and gradually increasing the speed. Once the cream turns to soft peaks, begin watching the cream carefully. A few minutes more, and the cream will stiffen. At this point, partially cover the top of the bowl with a draped kitchen towel to prevent splatter. Continue whisking on medium-high speed. Eventually the cream will separate into liquid and solid.

Strain the butter from the liquid and transfer the solid butter to your kitchen counter. Knead the butter on a flour sack towel for a bit to work out the remaining liquid, and then wrap the butter in a cheesecloth, shape it into either a roll or block, and store.

SMOKED OIL

Smoking oil is a great way to add depth to your food. Imagine a vinegar-and-oil salad dressing or fish poached in smoked oil. The technique is simple and full of options. Here's our favorite.

You'll need a deep-walled roasting pan, a bowl large enough to hold your oil but not as tall as the roasting pan, and a flameproof cup. Place the bowl and the cup centered inside of the roasting pan, each spread apart from the other by at least an inch. Put a neutral cooking oil, like rice bran, canola, or grapeseed, inside the bowl. In the flameproof cup, insert wood shavings along with green cardamom and whole cloves. You can put whichever spices (or pine needles) you wish in the cup, as long as they're fragrant while burning. Ignite the wood with a lighter until the flame burns without extinguishing. Melt a few tablespoons of butter in the microwave. Pour the butter on top of the flames, dousing the flames completely. Dousing in butter gives a stronger, longer-lasting aroma. Quickly and securely cover the roasting pan with first foil and then plastic wrap. Make sure the pan is closed airtight. Let the pan rest for 3 hours or up to overnight. Remove the oil from the pan and enjoy.

AGAVE PICKLES

In early summer, the agave plants start blossoming and if you catch them at the right time, you can pick the flowers as they turn yellow-orange but before they start to open. Once open, the flower buds begin to harden and become inedible in texture and flavor.

450 g (2 cups) unopened agave
    blossoms, cleaned (p. 203)
375 ml (1½ cups) apple cider
    vinegar
250 ml (1 cup) water
1 tbsp pickling salt
2 tbsp peppercorns
1 tsp mustard seeds
1 garlic clove, peeled
1 bay leaf

Trim the agave blossoms to the buds, leaving no stem, and place in a clamping Mason jar. In a medium saucepan, combine the vinegar, water, and pickling salt. Bring to a simmer. In a bowl, gather peppercorns, mustard seeds, garlic, and bay leaf. Add the spices to the Mason jar. Pour the boiled liquid over the blossoms and spice mixture and clamp shut. Let cool to room temperature for 1 hour, then chill.

POPPY SEED CAVIAR

Gathering wild poppy seeds is punishing work. Really. It's very tiring work that's hard on the hands. But wild poppy seeds, nearly twice the size of store-bought ones, are so much more exciting in flavor and texture. Caution: limit your intake, as they do have an intoxicating effect if overconsumed. I don't eat more than a few tablespoons at a sitting.

125 ml (½ cup) rice wine vinegar
65 ml (¼ cup) apple cider
    vinegar
55 g (¼ cup) sugar
1 tsp salt
375 ml (¾ cup) water
100 g (½ cup) poppy seeds
    (p. 204)

In a saucepan, combine all ingredients. Bring to a simmer, stirring occasionally. Simmer for 30 minutes or until the seeds remain firm but pop when you bite them. Remove from heat and store in an airtight container, refrigerated, for up to 2 weeks.

VEGETABLE SOILS

Eyebrows always rise when I tell a customer that they're eating soil. And while I do serve dirt (in the form of kaolin clay), soils are actually just a culinary concoction that resembles a soil's texture. We love kale, beet, and carrot soils the most because of their vibrant colors, but any colorful fruit or vegetable juice will do.

100 g (1 cup) almond meal or flour
56 g (¼ cup) butter, room temperature
65 ml (¼ cup) beet juice
2 tbsp dehydrated beet powder
½ tsp salt

Preheat the oven to 225°F.

Combine almond meal or flour, butter, and beet juice in a mixing bowl and cream the mixture with a rubber spatula. Spread the mixture on a Silpat-lined baking sheet to a ⅛-inch thickness. Bake for 20 to 30 minutes, being sure to not allow the dough to brown. Remove from the oven and immediately add the beet powder and salt. Crumble between the palms of your hands and let cool to room temperature. Store in an airtight container for up to 2 weeks.

INGREDIENT AVAILABILITY

All geographic data is provided by the USDA (www.plants.usda.gov)

ACORN (OAK)
GEOGRAPHY: All of North America
SUBSTITUTION: Almond, pecan, or hazelnut
OTHER ACCESS: Online, Asian markets that carry
  Korean products
ACCESS RATING: Easy

AGAVE
GEOGRAPHY: Southwest and southern United
  States
SUBSTITUTION: None
OTHER ACCESS: None
ACCESS RATING: Difficult

AMARANTH
GEOGRAPHY: All of North America
SUBSTITUTION: None
OTHER ACCESS: Online and in natural food stores
ACCESS RATING: Easy

BLACK CURRANT
GEOGRAPHY: Most of North America
SUBSTITUTION: Blueberry, blackberry
OTHER ACCESS: Online in purée or jelly form or in
  international markets with British foods
ACCESS RATING: Moderate

BULB PANICGRASS
GEOGRAPHY: Southwest
SUBSTITUTION: Any local wild grass identified
  through local extension office
OTHER ACCESS: None
ACCESS RATING: Moderate

CATTAIL (STALK, POLLEN)
GEOGRAPHY: All of North America
SUBSTITUTION: Cucumber for stalk
OTHER ACCESS: Pollen can be purchased from
  some tribal communities
ACCESS RATING: Easy

CHOLLA
GEOGRAPHY: Southwest
SUBSTITUTION: None
OTHER ACCESS: Online and in many Hispanic
  markets
ACCESS RATING: Moderate/difficult

CRAWFISH
GEOGRAPHY: All of North America
SUBSTITUTION: Shrimp
OTHER ACCESS: Available in most grocery stores
ACCESS RATING: Easy

DANDELION

GEOGRAPHY: All of North America
SUBSTITUTION: None
OTHER ACCESS: Online and natural food stores
ACCESS RATING: Easy

ELK

GEOGRAPHY: Western half of North America
SUBSTITUTION: Venison, beef
OTHER ACCESS: Online and through restaurant suppliers
ACCESS RATING: Moderate

FOUR-WING SALTBUSH

GEOGRAPHY: Western half of North America
SUBSTITUTION: Salt
OTHER ACCESS: None
ACCESS RATING: Difficult

GOAT

GEOGRAPHY: All of North America
SUBSTITUTION: Lamb
OTHER ACCESS: Middle Eastern markets, halal markets, and butcher shops
ACCESS RATING: Moderate/Easy

GRAPE (WILD)

GEOGRAPHY: All of the United States and the eastern half of Canada
SUBSTITUTION: None
OTHER ACCESS: Online
ACCESS RATING: Easy

HACKBERRY

GEOGRAPHY: All of the United States and the eastern half of Canada
SUBSTITUTION: Dates
OTHER ACCESS: None
ACCESS RATING: Moderate

HOREHOUND

GEOGRAPHY: All of North America
SUBSTITUTION: None
OTHER ACCESS: Online and natural food stores
ACCESS RATING: Easy

HOPS

GEOGRAPHY: Western half of the United States
SUBSTITUTION: None
OTHER ACCESS: Online through beer-making suppliers and natural food stores
ACCESS RATING: Easy

JAVELINA

GEOGRAPHY: Southwest
SUBSTITUTION: Boar, pork
OTHER ACCESS: None
ACCESS RATING: Difficult

JUNIPER

GEOGRAPHY: All of North America
SUBSTITUTION: None
OTHER ACCESS: Common in grocery stores
ACCESS RATING: Easy

MESQUITE

GEOGRAPHY: Southwest
SUBSTITUTION: None
OTHER ACCESS: Online and in natural food stores
ACCESS RATING: Moderate/easy

POPOTILLO

GEOGRAPHY: Southwest
SUBSTITUTION: None
OTHER ACCESS: Online
ACCESS RATING: Moderate/difficult

POPPY SEEDS

GEOGRAPHY: Most of North America
SUBSTITUTION: None
OTHER ACCESS: Grocery store
ACCESS RATING: Easy

PRICKLY PEAR

GEOGRAPHY: Most of North America, although most prolific in southern regions

SUBSTITUTION: None

OTHER ACCESS: Online, Hispanic markets, and most chain super markets carry the fruit and paddles in the produce section

ACCESS RATING: Easy

RABBIT

GEOGRAPHY: All of North America

SUBSTITUTION: Chicken

OTHER ACCESS: Online and in most butcher shops or Asian markets

ACCESS RATING: Moderate

RUSSIAN OLIVES

GEOGRAPHY: All of North America except the Southeast

SUBSTITUTION: Kalamata olives

OTHER ACCESS: None

ACCESS RATING: Difficult

SASSAFRAS

GEOGRAPHY: Eastern two-thirds of North America

SUBSTITUTION: None

OTHER ACCESS: Online and natural food stores

ACCESS RATING: Easy

SPRUCE

GEOGRAPHY: All of North America, most common at higher or wetter climates

SUBSTITUTION: Other conifer species

OTHER ACCESS: None

ACCESS RATING: Moderate

STINGING NETTLE

GEOGRAPHY: All of North America (except Arkansas—odd!)

SUBSTITUTION: Spinach

OTHER ACCESS: None

ACCESS RATING: Moderate

SUMAC

GEOGRAPHY: West of the Mississippi and parts of the East coast

SUBSTITUTION: Dried lemon zest ground with annatto

OTHER ACCESS: Middle Eastern markets and online

ACCESS RATING: Easy

WALNUTS (BLACK)

GEOGRAPHY: All of North America east of Colorado

SUBSTITUTION: Other species of walnut are found throughout all of North America

OTHER ACCESS: Online

ACCESS RATING: Easy

WINTERGREEN

GEOGRAPHY: All of North America except the Southeastern states

SUBSTITUTION: Any variety of mint

OTHER ACCESS: Grocery stores

ACCESS RATING: Easy

YUCCA

GEOGRAPHY: Most of North America, although most prolific in the southern region

SUBSTITUTION: None

OTHER ACCESS: None

ACCESS RATING: Moderate/difficult

ACKNOWLEDGMENTS

For a chef to step out of the kitchen long enough to write a book, there are many people who help make it happen. First and foremost is the amazing team at The Curious Kumquat, led by Sonia Guadiana—who knows my creations like no other.

And thanks to the many people who have shaped me into what I have become, even though I haven't met most of them—the eGullet community, especially Edsel Little, John Sconzo, Xianhang Zhang, Robert McWhirter, RJ Wong, Kerry Beal, the Chocolate Doctor, and Ruth Kendrick among many others. And the town of Silver City, a little oasis nestled in the middle of nowhere in New Mexico, nurtured my passion and allowed my creativity.

A special thanks to the local artists whose creations adorn these pages through Jay's photographs: Suzi Calhoun (dishes), Janey Katz (metal work), Phoebe Lawrence (dishes); and to Bauscher USA and Steelite USA for amazing dishes to plate my food.

Thanks to the gears behind the machine—Tom Hester, Nancy Smith, Pat Cusick, and the three Bens, who turned a chef's chicken-scratch into readable prose. David Squire, who led the brigade in the early design phase and showed us what the book could be. And to Michael Humphries, for web support.

And to family and family of choice—my mom, Peg, who always fed me great food from scratch; Tyler, my spouse, who tolerates the long hours of restaurant work, all of my harebrained ideas, and the ridiculousness of some of my food, and yet champions all of my quirks; Chuck and Judy, who gave us the means to create the impossible; and David, Betty, and Gary, who threw us some bones just at the right time. Who knew a James Beard–recognized restaurant could exist in the remoteness of the Gila Wilderness? They did. And to Zora O'Neill, who "discovered" me on a wandering tour with her mom back in 2010.

My time in New Orleans was surely the most influential for me. I'm forever indebted to Auntie Young, Miss Gloria, and Cooter Brown's cheese fries with a bottle of Mamba beer with Oz and Fry.

Last, but most importantly, to Andrea and Jay, who hung in there 'til the end to make this book happen. And to Lilly Ghahremani, who saw the potential and found us just the right publishing partner. And to Nicole Frail and our newfound friends at Skyhorse Publishing.

There is an elk steak with a dollop of acorn espuma waiting for all of you!

RESOURCES

ANSON MILLS
www.ansonmills.com
(803) 467-4122
Farro and a variety of other reclaimed heirloom grains

ART & CONVERSATION
www.lizardbreathranch.com
Ceramic dishes and art

BAUSCHER USA
www.bauscherInc.com
(919) 844-2801
Restaurant-quality dishes

DOUG SIMONS/CHANCHKA REMEDIES
www.chanchka.com
Wildcrafting and foraging workshops

KL KELLER FOOD WAYS
www.klkellerfoodways.com
(510) 740-2030
LeBlanc oil importer

KORIN JAPANESE TRADING CORP.
www.korin.com
(800) 626-2172
Chiba turning slicer, beautiful plating dishes

PHOEBE LAWRENCE
www.clayfulhands.com
Functional dishes and ceramics

MONTEREY BAY SPICE COMPANY
www.Herbco.com
(800) 500-6148
Kaolin and numerous herbs and spices including some
    foraged items

MONTICELLO BALSAMIC
www.OrganicBalsamic.com
New Mexico organic balsamic vinegar

PACARI
www.pacari.com
Biodynamic raw cacao products

RARE TEA CELLAR
www.rareteacellar.com
(773) 561-3000
Okinawa black sugar and a variety of extremely unique
    ingredients

SILVER CLOUD ESTATES – Maresh, Aleppo
www.silvercloudestates.com
(410) 565-6600
Marash and Aleppo pepper flakes and a variety of
    high-quality extracts

STEELITE USA
www.steelite.com
(800) 367-3493
Restaurant-quality dishes

SUE CHIN
www.buyacornflour.com
(925) 372-7177
Acorn flour

TERRA SPICE COMPANY
www.terraspicecompany.com
(574) 222-2462
A variety of chiles, spices, and molecular gastronomy
    ingredients

TONEWOOD MAPLE
www.ToneWoodMaple.com
(855) 755-5434
Maple syrup and flakes

SUGGESTED READING

Angier, Bradford. *Field Guide to Edible Wild Plants*. 2nd ed. Mechanicsburg, PA: Stackpole Books, 2008.

Ballerini, Luigi, and Ada De Santis. *A Feast of Weeds: A Literary Guide to Foraging and Cooking Wild Edible Plants*. Berkeley, CA: University of California Press, 2012.

Boutenko, Sergei. *Wild Edibles: A Practical Guide to Foraging, With Easy Identification of 60 Edible Plants and 67 Recipes*. Berkeley, CA: North Atlantic Books, 2013.

Elias, Thomas and Dykeman, Peter. *Edible Wild Plants: A North American Field Guide to Over 200 Natural Foods*. New York: Sterling, 2009.

Green, Connie, and Sarah Scott. *The Wild Table: Seasonal Foraged Food and Recipes*. New York: Viking Studio/Penguin Group, 2010.

Lyle, Katie Letcher. *Complete Guide to Edible Wild Plants, Mushrooms, Fruits, and Nuts: How to Find, Identify, and Cook Them*. 2nd ed. Guilford, CT: FalconGuides, 2010.

Moerman, Daniel E. *Native American Medicinal Plants: An Ethnobotanical Dictionary*. Portland, OR: Timber Press, 2009.

Peterson, Lee. *A Field Guide to Wild Edible Plants*. New York: Houghton Mifflin Harcourt, 1999.

Shaw, Hank. *Hunt, Gather, Cook: Finding the Forgotten Feast*. Emmaus, PA: Rodale Books, 2012.

Shufer, Vickie. *The Everything Guide to Foraging: Identifying, Harvesting, and Cooking Nature's Wild Fruits and Vegetables*. Avon, MA: Adams Media, 2011.

Thayer, Samuel. *The Forager's Harvest: A Guide to Identifying, Harvesting, and Preparing Wild Edible Plants*. Wisconsin: Forager's Harvest Press, 2006.

Turner, Nancy J. and Adam F. Szczawinski. *Common Poisonous Plants and Mushrooms of North America*. Portland, OR: Timber Press, 2003.

INDEX

100-Layer Sumac Apples, 156

METRIC CONVERSIONS

If you're accustomed to using metric measurements, use these handy charts to convert the imperial measurements used in this book.

Weight (Dry Ingredients)

1 oz		30 g
4 oz	¼ lb	120 g
8 oz	½ lb	240 g
12 oz	¾ lb	360 g
16 oz	1 lb	480 g
32 oz	2 lb	960 g

Volume (Liquid Ingredients)

½ tsp		2 ml
1 tsp		5 ml
1 Tbsp	½ fl oz	15 ml
2 Tbsp	1 fl oz	30 ml
¼ cup	2 fl oz	60 ml
⅓ cup	3 fl oz	80 ml
½ cup	4 fl oz	120 ml
⅔ cup	5 fl oz	160 ml
¾ cup	6 fl oz	180 ml
1 cup	8 fl oz	240 ml
1 pt	16 fl oz	480 ml
1 qt	32 fl oz	960 ml

Oven Temperatures

Fahrenheit	Celsius	Gas Mark
225°	110°	¼
250°	120°	½
275°	140°	1
300°	150°	2
325°	160°	3
350°	180°	4
375°	190°	5
400°	200°	6
425°	220°	7
450°	230°	8

Length

¼ in	6 mm
½ in	13 mm
¾ in	19 mm
1 in	25 mm
6 in	15 cm
12 in	30 cm